Dress to Impress
How a Navy Blazer Changed My Life

Second Edition

By Joyce Nelson Shellhart
founder of *Ready for Success*

Live Oak Publications

Cover & Layout Designer: Terin Martin
Editor: Keri Stifter
Illustrator: Lana k. Beck
Author Photo: Elizabeth Alcorn-Allen

ISBN 978-0-911781-21-2
Copyright © 2012 Joyce Nelson Shelhart

Second Edition
Previous Edition 2005

Live Oak Publications
An Imprint of Finney Company
8075 215th Street West
Lakeville, Minnesota 55044
www.finneyco.com
www.newcareerscenter.com

Printed in the United Sates of America

Dedication
With all my love -
Kiley, Jack, Andrew, Henry, Leo,
Elsa, and Norah
Keep your eyes open to all the possibilities!

Acknowledgements

How can I possibly acknowledge all the wonderful people involved with this book and my life? For truly without the support of so many this book would not exist because my life would have been much different.

Thank you, Lana. Your artwork and the story of your creative life is an inspiration to me. I am honored that you have blessed this book with your talents.

Al, your staff at Finney, and Keri Stifter have brought my words to the page in a book all of us can be proud of. And special thank you to Vicki Lansky who first saw the potential of the story.

Thank you Bobbi Dahlstrom of SeilerSchindel, PLLC, for your advice.

Liz Allen of Liz Allen Photography - the photo shoot was fun.

To my practice-writing group at Banfill-Locke Center for the Arts. Week in and week out you keep reminding me to put my butt in the chair and write.

To Sue Veazie, Gary Veazie, Clarice Schultz Nelson, Vera Brown, Joanne Funch, Betsy Lippert, Char Wilkinson, Jen, Pat, Bev, Dick, and an amazing list of women and men at *Ready for Success*. The list is long and filled with people who understood the problem and stepped forward to help.

To the clients of *Ready for Success* and my workshops, I learned more from you than you will ever know.

The Scott County Work Force Center: Diana and Shelley, I am honored that my workshops have been a part of your dynamic services for so many years.

Trinity Episcopal Church in Excelsior, Minnesota, there are not enough words to express my feelings of love for my "church family." You have been the base for not only *Ready for Success* but my life as it is today.

My "girlfriends" who coffee, lunch, and most of all listen, Kathy, Donna, Jan, Cheryl, Mel, Connie, Cyd, and the list grows, expands, and encircles those special relationships between women.

Panera Bread for allowing writers to crawl into a booth for hours and with a cup of coffee and a shortbread cookie immerse themselves in writing.

I would be remiss without commenting on my favorite department store, VON MAUR. Thank you for the service that has disappeared in so many others. Check out their sale racks. It is worth your effort.

And finally to my family….Our children and grandchildren, my sistas and brother, Mom, and most especially my husband Bruce. Thank you for shooing me out the door "to write." I love you.

How a Navy Blazer Changed My Life

Once upon a time, there was a young woman in college.

She met a young man. On the first night he told her he would marry her. She laughed and replied, "No way," but she was intrigued and flattered.

He became her constant companion.

He liked to drink, but it was college and who didn't?

He would get a little jealous…well, maybe a lot jealous. But that only meant he loved her.

He wanted to know her every move when he wasn't around. After a while she was careful whom she would mention she had seen at study group or for coffee after class. But that only meant he loved her.

They married two weeks after she graduated from college.

In a few years they had their first daughter.

He still drank quite a bit. She had quit; she didn't really enjoy drinking and the fights that would erupt.

He was jealous, suspicious, and critical. He called her stupid and ugly. But he only said and did those things because he loved her and he wanted to help her.

She was diagnosed with a chronic illness after their second daughter was born. Now she was lazy.

The years passed, and she tried hard not to evoke his anger. After all, it was her fault if he got mad and put his fist through the door. The next time it could be her head.

One day he poked his finger so hard into her chest while yelling at her, it left bruises for days. He was sorry afterwards.

He told her it was her fault for making him so mad. She accepted what he said as truth.

The next time he pushed her down. He claimed she was so clumsy that she tripped. How could anyone that stupid, ugly, and lazy be so clumsy too?

He loved her and was only trying to help her.

She never dressed up. If she did, he would question her. Who was she trying to impress? Did she have a boyfriend?

One day he was yelling at their teenage daughter. His accusations about her behavior, her clothing, and her friends sounded too familiar— and totally unacceptable.

That was the day she woke up.

It was hard to face the truth about my life, especially after being in a relationship for 20 years. It was even more difficult for my children, teenage daughters who were facing their own choices in relationships. Their future was the biggest reason I made the decisions I did. I know personally how choices repeat themselves in families, and I wanted more for my daughters. I realized I had married a man just like my stepfather. I had hated it when he said hurtful, demeaning things to me, yet here I was, allowing my husband to say those same things to our daughter. And she believed it must be okay; she had, after all, heard him say those things to me. It had to stop and it had to stop now!

During the process of removing the "wasband's" (my now ex-husband's) negative influence from my life, I looked at how I presented myself to the world. I decided I wanted to wear something more than just jeans and t-shirts. I had been a high school art teacher, and every year on my annual evaluation I received one negative comment: DOES NOT DRESS APPROPRIATELY FOR THE JOB.

I began watching my friends in church. What did they wear that helped them create an appearance of success and confidence? For some reason I knew a navy blazer would change my life. I was in the process of a divorce, concerned about losing my home, had a small disability income, and certainly couldn't afford a new blazer. Besides, my teenage daughters needed things more. I began searching Goodwill and thrift shops for an inexpensive, gently used navy blazer. I was a size 20–22, and finding something to fit me that wasn't worn out or clown-like was a real challenge. I finally found my navy blazer. I put it on over the same jeans and t-shirt that the week before I had worn to my women's group at church.

"Joyce, did you cut your hair?"

"Did you lose weight?"

"You look great!"

The only thing different was the navy blazer. After years of negative comments, I needed those positive words. I wanted more of this affirming stuff; it was like a drug for my soul.

Making the change was not easy. Fortunately, my friends were supportive. However, my children repeated the same question their father had asked:

"Who do you think you are?"

I slipped on the navy blazer to go to a high school conference for my youngest daughter, then a freshman. "You're going like that?" she asked. Fast-forward four years, when I went to a school conference for my now senior daughter. I put on a nice pair of khakis and a sweater. Her question again was, "You're going like that?" But this time she expected to see me present myself in a more professional manner.

I remember trying out a scarf around my neck for the first time—tying and retying it in front of the mirror for twenty minutes. When I came out of the bathroom, my daughters laughed and said, "Who are you trying to impress?" I just put my shoulders back and walked out the door. I knew then who I needed to impress:

MYSELF.

Table of Contents

Introduction

*The fact is people treat you as **they perceive** you to be.
That perception has a lot to do with what you look like and how you
present yourself.*

I remember being told you have 16–18 seconds to make a first impression. I still see that number quoted. A few years ago the accepted time became 6–8 seconds. I haven't done the research, but I think it is less than that. How long does it take you to click through 200 channels and know there is not a thing on television you want to watch? We make quick decisions all day long; we don't take the time to linger over them.

Success Secret #1
Make your first impression count! Do you want to spend the rest of the interview climbing up out of the hole your first impression put you in?

I have met some amazing women on my journey. Many people have shared with me their personal stories—stories that brought tears to my eyes—and yet to see these people today, to know the struggles they have encountered to learn to present themselves in a whole new light, is awe-inspiring. I don't claim to know everything there is to know about personal presentation, but I am here to share my success. In fact, if you have lunch with me, you may be amazed to discover that when I am talking, I put my elbows on the table. I lean in and listen with my full being. This is a habit I have tried many times to break, but I've finally learned to accept it about myself and actually like it for being part of who I am.

My mother was widowed twice. She worked in a factory to support five children in the 1960s and 1970s. In her young adult life she had actually done some modeling. However, the need to put food on the table for hungry children forced her to seek a more stable occupation. Most of my youth she wore jeans, t-shirts, and heavy shoes to work. She sewed much of her non-work clothing as well as ours. I remember being embarrassed by my hand-sewn clothing and hand-me-downs from family friends. Eventually I felt I wasn't very good at selecting clothing. When I married and my "wasband" questioned my clothing choices, I had even less confidence in my ability to choose the right things to wear.

So how did I begin to change my personal appearance? I purchased a gently used navy blazer and...

- threw it on over jeans and a t-shirt.
- wore it with a pair of khakis and a turtleneck.
- folded a large square scarf in a triangle, draped it around my shoulders over the blazer, and put the ends under the lapel. I then wore the blazer over a blouse with a simple skirt or slacks.
- draped a large square scarf folded in a triangle over my shoulder under my brastrap, put the blazer on over the scarf, and buttoned the blazer. The scarf had a blouse effect.
- wore it with a small square scarf around my throat, either off to one side or in the middle, when wearing jeans and a t-shirt.
- put it on over a dress. If the dress was a color other than navy, I draped a long scarf under my lapel using the navy in the blazer and the dress color to tie the look together.

My first step was to choose my base color: navy blue. It was the beginning for me. I searched garage sales, estate sales, and clearance racks for very low-cost accessories to go with navy, such as scarves, jewelry, turtlenecks, blouses, shoes, and handbags. In a matter of months, I had built an entire wardrobe around one color—and basically one item of clothing. Needless to say, I quickly wore out that blazer. Now that I felt more self-assured about what I wanted, when my sister asked what I would like for my birthday I confidently replied, "a new navy blazer!"

I am an inch taller today, and to be honest, women in my age group don't normally grow one inch. I suspect I only stand taller with more confidence and self-assurance. Knowing you are dressed appropriately for the situation allows you to concentrate on other things, such as conversation, work, and being in the moment.

In the Beginning
In December of 1996, while channel surfing (I had gotten custody of the remote and the recliner in the divorce!), I happened across a short piece on a TV news magazine about the Bottomless Closets organization in Chicago that provided interview-appropriate clothing for low-income women. I awoke the next morning, sat down at a used computer recently given to me by a friend, and wrote a business plan for what I would need to make happen to begin such an organization. I had no previous experience in business or the non-profit world, other than as a volunteer and client. I was on disability from teaching due to multiple sclerosis and in the midst of an ugly divorce. In hindsight it is no wonder people would sometimes look at me with amazement when I was so articulate about what the organization should look like. I knew from my personal experience that there was a need—not only for the clothing but also for guidance.

In 1997, a group of volunteers from Trinity Episcopal Church in Excelsior, Minnesota, and I formed *Ready for Success.* We opened our doors in November of 1997 in the parish hall. We began as an outreach project of our church. Most of our early volunteers were members of the church and their friends. We were open four days a month, by appointment only, and we saw clients only upon referral.

Ready for Success was formed to provide low-income women in the Minneapolis/St. Paul area with a free clothing resource for interviews and the workplace. Each client received the one-on-one attention of a volunteer personal shopper who helped her "shop the racks" of gently used clothing. The two would spend about two hours shopping for four outfits including shoes, handbag, bra, underwear, scarves, and jewelry—whatever items she needed for her personal situation. In the winter, if we were lucky we'd even find her a coat. Each client was invited to return for an additional two visits, though we encouraged her to save one appointment for another season, as helping her develop a four-season wardrobe was necessary in Minnesota. During the "shopping trips" the client and her personal volunteer shared many ideas, tips, and suggestions about the workplace. As Sue Veazie, my good friend and current program director of *Ready for Success*, said, "It is not about the clothes. It is so much more."

This shopping experience separated Ready for Success from some other clothing closet programs, where the volunteers shop the racks and bring brought the clothing to the clients to try on. We felt many woman needed the shopping experience to give them confidence when shopping beyond our doors. We were asked many times if we offered resume and job hunting skills. We tried those things, but those services were offered many other places; we provided an important service that was lacking at other agencies. Our choice to specialize in our niche allowed our referring agencies to expand their offerings to clients without the floor space a service like *Ready for Success* demands.

The women who come to *Ready for Success* are from shelters for battered women, welfare-to-work programs, recovery programs, ex-offender programs, refugee programs, job skills and work readiness programs, dislocated worker programs, and displaced home-maker programs.

The Success of *Ready for Success*

- In November of 1997, *Ready for Success* opened its doors at Trinity Episcopal Church in Excelsior, Minnesota.
- In 1999, because of construction at Trinity Church, *Ready for Success* moved to a larger space in Minnetonka, Minnesota, allowing more appointment times with a growing volunteer base beyond the parish community.
- In 2001, *Ready for Success* joined Episcopal Community Services, a statewide social service organization, offering more opportunity for expansion and support.
- In January of 2003, *Ready for Success* opened a second site on the East Side of St. Paul, Minnesota, at Hazel Park United Church of Christ.
- In January of 2004, *Ready for Success*, West moved to a larger site offered by St. Mark's Episocopal Cathedral in Minneapolis.
- In 2009, Episcpal Community Services partnering with Goodwill Easter Seals opened *Men's Ready for Success*, based on the same principles of the women's program.
- In 2010, both programs moved to larger sites.

The *Ready for Success* programs so far have served over 20,000 women and men. They currently average 2,000 clients a year from over 200 different agencies. This happens only with the hard work of over 300 volunteers: personal shoppers, clothing inventory specialists, fundraisers, clothing drive organizers, and many more. Clothing donors include individuals, businesses, and corporations that supply the hundreds of thousands of items that pass through the doors of *Ready for Success*. Financial donors have recognized the importance of *Ready for Success* and provide the much-needed financial support. Each piece of this amazing puzzle is *Ready for Success.*

When we first opened, I was constantly asked whether or not there was a need for a service such as this with the influence of business casual dress in the workplace. I think our growth and numbers answer that question very clearly—*YES!* As the pendulum has swung from business casual to more professional dress today the answer is an even more resounding *YES!*

I have been blessed to know and work with wonderful women at *Ready for Success*. By keeping my eyes and ears open, I have learned a lot. It was enlightening for me to discover women who I thought always looked so confident and "put together" still obsessed about whether what they were wearing was appropriate. Most relaxed over time as they learned and accepted that their personal choices were in line with what other women were wearing at work or to special events. How did they learn that? By watching, talking, and sharing with other women. That is what our concept of women helping other women is all about.

Women are always struggling with what is appropriate to wear in a given situation, especially…

- low-income women, who may know how to dress but can't afford it.
- women moving from very casual work environments (convenience stores, factories, etc.) to office settings.
- woman lacking experience and confidence in this area who are competing with others who have more "dressing for work" experience.
- woman coming from college and training programs where the dress attire is jeans and t-shirts.
- woman looking to change their self-image as well as their entire life.

The last situation is the most profound change a woman can make and the most amazing change to witness. Those of us at *Ready for Success* have been truly blessed to be part of these changes made by the women we work with. I am not claiming that an improved wardrobe and personal presentation will get you a job you are not qualified for, help you keep a job to which you consistently arrive late, or get the promotion you don't deserve. But presenting yourself in a professional manner—in combination with skill, desire, and a positive attitude, will help you achieve great things. And that I know from personal experience.

This book is to help address the situations I have seen come up repeatedly in over 15 years of speaking about *Ready for Success* and dressing for the workplace:

- "I wish someone would talk to my entry-level employees about how to dress appropriately!"
- "I wish someone would talk to my daughter, who has just graduated from college and is getting started in the workplace, about how she should dress!"
- "I wish I could get my clients going into the banking skills training program to see how important it is to dress the part!"

Many women I work with find clothing choices as a way to rebel against parents or mothers who dress very well. Others do not have a role model of a working professional woman to emulate. Still others use "business casual" as a way to avoid worrying about their appearance. Many of them have confided in me that they do wish they knew how to present themselves better and with more confidence.

So here it is—a book with some things your mother probably told you but you weren't listening; some things your mother didn't know and maybe you want to share with her; some new things to help you get the positive encouragement we all need.

If someone has left this book lying on your desk, don't take offense. He or she must feel you are worth the effort and may be trying to tell you your personal appearance is holding you back from reaching new levels of success. If this book is a gift, say thank you, for the giver believes you are capable of much more, and just knowing someone believes in us can be a powerful force in our lives.

I struggled whether there was a reason to rewrite *Dress to Impress*. Was there still a need for this little book? Then I was doing a workshop at a workforce center, and I looked around the room at how the clients were dressed.

"How do you dress when you go to the grocery store?" I asked.

One young woman laughed nervously, "Like this, sweats and t-shirts, and I have been known to leave the house in my fuzzy pink slippers for a quick milk and bread run."

"What if you found yourself in line behind the sister of your best friend from high school? You haven't seen her for years. The usual banter occurs, and then she asks the question: What are you up to these days? Now you have a choice. You can lie and say everything is great! I love my job! Or you can tell the truth. I like what I do, but I would LOVE to find another position with more responsibility; or, I am job hunting and hoping to _____. You fill in the blank. Your next job or first job likely lies within the circle of people you know or, even more likely, within the circle of someone you know. This is networking. So what if this woman is standing there thinking…I know so and so, but do I want to recommend 'fuzzy slippers' here?"

Job-hunting is a full-time job. And the most important thing you have to sell is yourself! Be Prepared!

Right now you can go to dozens, probably hundreds, of websites and blogs that will offer tips on dressing for the workplace. I have spent hours exploring these sites and walked away with my head spinning from all the information. That is my point. I decided *Dress to Impress* could be your guide to help you narrow your search for YOUR perfect look. I cannot possibly tell you all there is to know about the subject, but I can give you a place to start. If you find something that you want more information about, hop onto that information highway and expand your knowledge. But, beware, look where the information is coming from; how reliable is the resource?

In the same workshop I asked the participants to consider how they looked when they went house hunting. Finding affordable, suitable rental property can be difficult in a tight market. Be sure the future landlord's first impression of you is one of someone who takes care of himself or herself and thus would take care of his/her property.

Your life is an amazing journey! Go first class! For 20 years I thought my abusive "wasband" and multiple sclerosis were keeping me in the baggage compartment. One day I discovered it was me. I held the key all along! So what is holding you back from climbing up out of the baggage compartment and into first class? Who is the person you see in the mirror? That person is capable of amazing things. *Go get them!*

Joyce Nelson Shellhart

CHAPTER ONE

WHY?

"I can't afford to dress like that!"
"It's more important who I am on the inside!"
"It's a bunch of old lady clothes!"
"Thank goodness I own my own business. I don't have to
 dress like that!"

I have heard all these excuses and even said them myself.
As I look back, I realize I said many of those things because I was
scared.

- I was scared I would "do it wrong."
- I was scared of the reaction of other people within my family
  and friend circle. (Let's be honest; I was only scared of my "wasband's" reaction.)
- I was scared to look in the mirror and see the person who could
  do things I was too frightened to do.

So let's face these fears, one at a time.

I can't afford to dress like that!
This is the biggest reason I wrote Chapter 3, "It's a Work Uniform!" When we break down a "look" into simple pieces and a base
color, shopping becomes more specific. We no longer have to wan-
der among racks of clothes, overwhelmed with even the prospect
of where to start. Instead, we have a starting point, searching for a

certain color or piece of clothing. I am surprised when I'm at a speaking engagement how willing other women are to share their favorite consignment shops or thrift stores. And every time the rest of the audience will look surprised because the women who are giving them these tips are beautifully dressed and have the reputation for creating an image others want to emulate. The multibillion dollar fashion industry wants you always shopping for the newest fashion.....every season....every year. I say, okay, I'll add a new color of top over my black pants, when I find the piece on clearance or in the secondary market. But first I ask myself these questions:

- Does the "color of the season" look good on me? (Orange does not look good next to my face!)
- Does the latest fashion style work with my body type? (Belted dresses draw attention to an area of my body that is best underplayed!)
- Does the fashion statement make sense in my work environment? (Four-inch stiletto heels are not practical if you are standing all day at a customer service desk, nor are they practical for me with my MS balance issues.)

Unless you work in the fashion industry, wait and see if the fashion is enduring—or whether it makes sense. Otherwise start simple, so your first clothing investment is not out of style in a year or two.

It's more important who I am on the inside!

I said this to myself for years. But the reality is, when you meet someone for the first time, is he or she going to take the time to get to know you under your exterior presentation? I wish this wasn't the case. I wish each of us had a sign that flashed, "I am _____." Fill in the blank with all the positive things you want your prospective employer, client, landlord, colleague, supervisor, or potential networking connection to know about you in that first few seconds of meeting. Except you do walk around with a sign. How you present yourself carries a message:

- Do you care enough about wanting a job, house, or respect to put forth the effort it requires to dress for the part?
- Do you respect the other person enough to take the effort to show why he or she should be glad to hire you, connect with you, work with you, or rent to you?

Who you are on the inside is important. In my case, a wonderful, capable woman was buried under thick layers of low self-esteem. Putting on a navy blazer and looking in the mirror day after day slowly thinned those thick layers. I began to realize the only roadblocks in my life were ones I put there. There is always another choice, although it may not be easy. Dressing the part of a confident, capable woman helped me bring her out in the open and present her to the world.

It's a bunch of old lady clothes!

I'd be a wealthy woman if I had a dime for every time I have heard a woman, usually under 30, say that. You may not be happy with the current dress code, written or unwritten. But until you get into a position of power, you will probably not change the reality of the world today. Think of how many times you have heard in the news comments about how a woman in a position of power dresses—for example, Hillary Clinton's pantsuits or Michelle Obama's dresses. If these women who are successful and in positions of respect are still being judged on how they dress, do you really think it doesn't matter?

What I am proposing is a simplified way to dress for work. I am not telling you this is the way you should dress in your off time. And I'm not saying you will never get hired or promoted if you don't dress like this. But why limit your opportunities by how you present yourself? Do you think your friends will laugh? Let them laugh as you deposit your paycheck.

Thank goodness I own my own business. I don't have to dress like that!

This comment surprises me! You are your business. If you want to be taken seriously, you want to dress seriously. Think about it carefully. Your business will be judged by the way you present yourself. Even if you have no employees, you still need to look like the boss.

Now that we've done away with excuses, let's get started dressing to impress!

CHAPTER TWO

Developing a Sense of Style

Developing a sense of clothing style does not have to involve hours of study or years of experience. Pick any up-scale mall in a business area, preferably one with eating establishments—maybe even a nice sit-down restaurant or two. The regular suburban shopping mall will not provide the inspiration you need for a working wardrobe. You want to go where women in business grab a quick lunch, meet clients or one another for lunch, or do a little shopping. Around noon, get a cup of coffee, sit down on a bench, and pay attention to what people are wearing.

- Which women impress you as being successful?
- Can you guess the industries different individuals work in? Are they industries in which you are interested in working?
- Do some outfits use classic pieces?
- Remember to keep your body type in mind. Are there certain styles of clothing that would look better on you than others?
- What is your favorite outfit? Do you have anything in your closet that could duplicate the look?
- Notice details like jewelry and scarves. How do these things add to or detract from the overall look?
- Is there a recurring theme in shoes and handbags?

Fashion and Style

There is a difference between style and fashion. Fashion changes constantly with each new season and trend. Style is long-lasting. A wardrobe based on style will have classic pieces that will carry over from year to year, perhaps with a dash of new colors and accessories. Young women and women new to the workforce often desire the latest fashion trend, and their wardrobes quickly become dated. You don't have to completely exclude the latest fashion trends from your wardrobe. You can wear a "baby doll" cut top under a blazer or a cute wrap scarf—just mix it with simple classic pieces for your stylish statement.

Why is it important to know your body type?

Not all styles work well on all figures, which is why it's important for you to know your body type. If you don't, there are a wide variety of charts and measurements available to help you figure it out. Where you gain and lose weight can affect your shape. Your awareness of your shape can help you avoid spending money on clothing that will only hang in your closet unworn. When I was 16, I asked my mother why no one told my grandmother that pulling her pants up to her bosom was unattractive. Little did I realize that someday my waist and my bosom would be in the same place. I have lost a little weight now, but putting any emphasis on my waist is best avoided. I have family members with wonderful waistlines above generous, womanly hips; for them belted tunics and dresses are wonderful. Look in the Resources at the end of this book for my favorite website for helping women discover their body type; it also provides some tips with each type.

You CAN Shop When You Can't Buy

A free resource when you are seeking style ideas is a quality department store. This research expedition is best done by yourself without children or friends. It is too easy to become distracted. Avoid the junior, beach, golf wear, and athletic wear departments. Stroll through departments obviously geared toward the working woman, touching fabrics and observing the clothing selections displayed on mannequins. One of the things women tell me most often is that they never go into expensive department stores they can't afford because the clerks act mean or avoid them. Change your mind set!

Yes, you will be treated better and with more respect if you are clean and neat. Look directly at the clerk, smile, and say "no thanks" when asked if you need any help. I also freely admit I have found my very best bargains in the very best stores. You can find out more about that in Chapter 10.

As part of your research, see if you can find out the answers to these questions:

- What fit looks great on your body type? For example, does a short bolero jacket look good? Does a long jacket make you look short?
- What brands and what sizes in those brands are a great fit for you? Be ready to try on several different sizes. Size is just a number!
- What is the current blazer form, lapel shape, fabric, color, and color combination?

If the department isn't busy, go ahead and ask the sales associate her opinion, but remember you are not there to buy. Bring along a small notebook and pencil to jot down any brands you like and the sizes in that brand. This information will help when you are deciding on your "work uniform," which you will learn about in Chapter 3. For now, revel in seeing a new you looking back from the mirror. There is more to learn before you buy.

Fashion Fatalities

Skip most fashion magazines when you are looking for advice about business clothing. Their purpose is to sell the latest fashion, not help you move up in your career.

Beware fashion blogs that will link you to one of their sponsors. Their interest is not necessarily your interview, but only that you are wearing their sponsor's clothing to that interview.

Have you ever wondered how some of the women on television would actually perform the jobs their characters are supposed to have, dressed the way they are? I am thrilled to see women portraying characters in powerful positions, but do judges really wear plunging necklines on the bench?

I recently saw on television a young female attorney wearing a short skirt and provocative neckline while sliding her derrière across the desk of her colleague, a man wearing a three-piece suit. Remember, television shows are out to sell ratings, not reality.

In the following chapters, I will comment on many things concerning how to present yourself. But the one mistake I consistently hear young women are making at work is allowing their sexuality to enter the office. Whether you are conscious of it or not, many fashion trends are based on the premise that "sex sells." Save your low-cut tops, spaghetti straps, and extra-tight skirts or pants for going out after work. (See Chapter 4, "Daywear Versus Datewear.")

Look Around

Who impresses you where you work? I encourage women to dress like the women in leadership positions at their workplace. If there are no women in leadership positions, the men in those positions will give you a clue by how they dress. A business suit on a man equates a comparable look on a woman.

Watch people at social functions or your house of worship.

What are people wearing that impresses you? What are people wearing that doesn't impress you? Why?

Pay attention to what women are wearing in various businesses. What does the bank teller at your local bank wear? Is it any different from what the loan officer is wearing? What about the customer service representative at the local high-end department store? What is the receptionist wearing at the city office or county office? Most important of all, does what they are wearing say success?

Now that you have an idea of what you want—and what you don't want—when it comes to your look, turn to Chapter 3 to get started on choosing those classic pieces.

CHAPTER THREE

It's a Work Uniform!

This chapter is devoted to the beginner who is wondering, "Where do I even start?" Men actually have had this figured out for 200 years. They can begin with a navy suit, one or two other suits, a few shirts and ties, good shoes, and they are ready. They mix and match from their basics.

Many fashion experts consider what I am about to propose profanity, but then again, they don't work with women trying to get started on an entry-level salary or no salary. I suggest you start building a "work uniform" of a base color and basic pieces. Then as your confidence and your income grows, you can begin to develop your own style. So let's get started on that "work uniform."

Business casual has changed the look of the American workforce. It has allowed employees to come to work, in some businesses, quite literally in almost anything they please. It has opened the doors to more choices in clothing for the workplace. Some of those choices are good and some are not so good. The dress code, written and unwritten, can vary dramatically from business to business, and even from department to department. When you first start a new job, you should look around.

- How do other employees dress?
- How does management dress?
- Are there certain days when better dress is required?
- Is there a "casual Friday"?

Who is Your Employer?

While business casual may be a boon for employees, I have heard a number of business owners, upper-level management, and customers mourn the loss of professional business attire. When women tell me they no longer need suits or even blazers for their prospective jobs, I ask them several questions:

- Is the company owned or run by someone under 40?
  If so, it is possibly a very casual atmosphere.
- Is the business in the creative field such as public relations, advertising, or graphic design?
  If so, it is possibly more casual with a side of creativity and fun.
- Is the business in the financial field?
  If so, it is probably more conservative.
- Does someone on the East Coast own the company, or is someone from the East Coast a major stockholder in the business?
  If so, color choices are more limited to black and white and neutral.
- Does someone on the West Coast own the company, or is someone from the West Coast a major stockholder in the business?
  If so, it may have a very casual atmosphere.
- Does someone in mid-America own the company, or is someone from mid-America a major stockholder in the business?
  If so, it may have an environment that blends both coastal regions.
- Does someone from Europe own the business, or is someone from Europe a major stockholder in the company?
  If so, Europeans usually have a higher expectation of clothing quality and conservative dress.
- Is the business located in the suburbs, the city, or rural America?
  The more conservative dress is usually prevalent in the more populated areas. It is interesting to note that the public in some small towns is less accepting of very casual dress in their banks and white-collar businesses.

If a company's customer is uncomfortable with the way an employee presents herself or himself—and how the company is represented by its employee—this can have a negative effect on the bottom line of the business.

When I ask women about the expectations of their employers as far as dress is concerned, they'll often look at me blankly and say, "I don't know. I haven't thought about it." And that is exactly my point. Limiting yourself to YOUR idea of business casual limits your choices and often your opportunities.

Business Casual

Business casual today can vary from jeans with flannel shirts in the winter and t-shirts in the summer to men in suits who don't wear ties on Fridays. The dress code of the working woman has changed considerably over the last several decades. I remind women that in some form it still exists, although it is often unwritten.

Success Secret #4

Just as you would not consider wearing a McDonald's uniform out on a date, the clothes you wear to work are probably not what you will wear out with your friends or around the house. Your work wardrobe is what you need to gain positive strokes at work.

You may not need to wear a suit to work every day, but there are those special occasions when you'll need one—maybe a prospective new customer or an out-of-town buyer is coming into the office. Or there is the BIG meeting. You do need to know how to put on something more professional than business casual and feel confident and comfortable in what you are wearing.

Changes in Workplace Attire

Clothing choice	Pre-Business Casual	Post-Business Casual
Suits	Dark colors, blazer with skirt or pants of same fabric.	Almost any color goes, with some wonderful new easy-care fabrics.
Tops and blouses	Light neutral colors, usually silk, rayon, cotton, or polyesters.	Cotton t-shirts or turtlenecks worn under blazers, cardigans, or vests. Beautiful colored silk or great new easy-care manmade fabrics in blouses. Tailored blouses are also now worn open over a t-shirt or tank (not too revealing a tank) as a blazer effect.
Skirts	Knee-length or slightly longer. Not floor/ankle length for work.	Wide variety of choices, avoiding mini-length and slits to mid-thigh or above.
Pants	Dark, usually pleated in front.	Flat fronts with a wide variety of pant choices and lengths, avoiding shorts, capris, hems dragging on the floor, and blue jeans.

Blazers	Structured wider, thick shoulder pads, length reaching upper thigh or fingertip length with arms placed at side.	Unstructured with softer fabrics, structured short bolero length to almost knee length. A wide variety of lapel or no-lapel choices.

Says Who?

When I began dressing more professionally, I heard several things that I accepted as fact. I have since discovered the following "clothing myths" can be ignored when dressing for the workplace.

Blazers and pants or skirts must always be the same fabric.

Manufacturers tell us that. Why? So we buy more. I have had sales associates tell me I have to buy the matching skirt even though the blazer is the only piece on sale, and to be honest, the only piece I want. I do have a little rule of thumb when I am mixing different fabrics: Wear the heavier fabric on the bottom; our sense of proportion will accept that better.

Beware of matching blacks and matching navy blues.

This is true, but not to the extent some fashion experts will tell you. Again, if the colors are close, I prefer the darker on the bottom, as the eye accepts this as a nicer look. I will carry my selections from the closet to the window to double check how close in color they are or if the colors don't work at all. I have also encountered "black navy," the very dark navy that is nearly black. This is a difficult color to match accurately, but it carries off very well with either black or navy. Shades of black are more forgiving than some navy colors to match. In fact, it is acceptable to wear most shades of black together today.

Never wear white AFTER Labor Day, and wear white shoes ONLY between Easter or Memorial Day and Labor Day.

This myth has been dying a slow death. I have seen and worn some wonderful winter white suits. I do have a hard time wearing white shoes any time of the year, unless it is athletic shoes. They just make me feel that my size 8 shoes look much, much larger. Maybe I would feel differently if I was blessed with size 6 feet. Remember in developing your basic clothing plan that white can be harder to keep clean.

Belts, shoes, and handbags should all match.

Business casual has buried this one. In fact, currently it is much more fashionable to have a brightly colored handbag and more muted shoes, or the reverse—fun, bright shoes and a muted handbag. If you're blessed with a body type where belts look good on you, have fun with all the choices.

Your Basic Working Wardrobe

What to Look For:

- Pants and skirts in several weights and lengths in your base color. Your research in department stores and malls is helpful here, as you can find out what lengths are currently in fashion. Think about what you can do to modify skirts and pants you currently own. Hemming is the easiest.
- Blazers and cardigans that are either in your base color or complement your base color.
- Tops in your base color to create the two-color outfit or three-color outfit, and tops to complement your base color.
- Belts, shoes, and handbags in the base color.

This becomes the basis for your working wardrobe. Keeping to these simple choices in the beginning will simplify your shopping time, make the most out of your closet space, and make getting dressed for work much easier and less stressful. Next let's look at the specifics of these choices.

Success Secret #5
Choose a base color to work with. Black is probably the easiest and looks great on most women. (In hindsight I should have chosen black over navy when I began.)

Acquiring the Basics

I want to say a word here about choosing the base color. Black is the industry standard, and no matter what the latest fashion TV show, magazine, or blog says, it is the easiest. If you are blessed with wonderful autumn highlights or pale blonde hair and skin, browns or blues may be a better choice. We are a world populated with skin tones and hair colors of unbelievably beautiful combinations. Again, my intention here is to offer suggestions to women who are seeking entry into the sometimes confusing, bewildering, and terrifying world of personal presentation, and to reassure you it really is not rocket science. Get ready…get set…let's go! Follow these ideas, and you're in business!

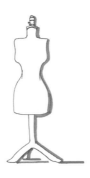

Pants

A basic pair of pants—black dress pants—is a good place to start. Flat fronts are more flattering. In fact, pleated fronts date your wardrobe. Dress pants don't feel like jeans. They should have a slightly looser feel, with fabric that nicely lies across your tummy area. Sometimes just moving the button over can make a pair of so-so pants perfect. Pants containing a small amount of spandex have a lot more give and can be very comfortable to wear. (I am not talking about spandex leggings for the office. This is exercise wear.) Be sure that any pockets on the side are not gapping open and that the zipper is lying flat. Back pockets can help or hurt the derrière (look from behind), depending on your body type. Is the crotch of the pants fitting where it should, or is it hanging two inches below or pulling up tightly behind? Check the waistband. Is it properly stitched? If it has elastic, does it appear to be in good shape? What about the width of the leg? Too wide or very narrow can quickly date a pair of pants. What about the fabric—how is it cared for? And you thought I was just going to say buy a pair of black pants!

Then find a nice pair of pants to complement your base color.

In your office, khakis or Dockers may be the standard pant of choice. They do come in great colors, including black. Even if khakis are the office norm, you still need to have a nice pair of dress pants. They can make that "career casual" impression. Over time, dark colored jeans have become more acceptable in some offices. Several years ago, I only owned one or two pairs of jeans. Today I own about five pairs of dark colored jeans. They can be the perfect accent for an evening out, paired with nice boots or heels. I have learned that jeans with spandex can be very deceiving. If they fit you perfectly in the dressing room, take home the next smaller size. Otherwise, within less than an hour, you will wish you had. Dark jeans are not acceptable for an interview. Even the most casual of work environments still demand at least khakis to make that great first impression.

Skirts

You should have in your wardrobe a basic skirt in the same color as your pants. Skirts can be tricky to figure out the front from the back. Normally the label goes in the back, but occasionally it's on the side. If there is a slit, it should open no higher than slightly above your knee. Try sitting down in front of a three-way mirror if you question this advice. That image usually convinces any woman I have worked with. You can lightly baste the slit closed to the knee for work and then open it back up for datewear. Frequently slits or pleats are tacked shut on the bottom of a new skirt. It is okay to open them. Skirts can be knee-length or slightly below, mid-calf length, or ankle length. I find skirts that hit across the heaviest part of the calf to be very unflattering. Either shorten them to the narrowing just above or lengthen them to just below the widest part of the calf for a nicer look. Thin straight skirts generally give a slimming look. Full skirts and pleats provide a more casual look. In northern climates, tights with skirts are a good choice in the winter. Leggings come and go on the fashion scene; they are more acceptable on young women, but never for an interview.

Split skirts go by several names, but they always border somewhere between pants and skirts. I personally love the look with a fashion boot. The split skirt should cover the top of the boot for the nicest line. It should swing a bit; in other words, it is not just a pair of shorts or capris over boots.

Jackets

A blazer in your base color and a second jacket in a complementary or neutral color are terrific starting points. Blazers or jackets have a wide range of styles and quality, thanks to business casual. If the pockets are sewn shut, leave them that way. It will prevent you from shoving your hands, keys, cell phones, and other things in them, keeping the jacket looking nice longer without sagging pockets. Clip the threads to open the back pleat if it is tacked shut on a new jacket. Try on a wide variety of blazer lengths. This is easy to do on your research trip through a fine department store. When you see one at a thrift store or garage sale you will already have some idea of the length and style you are looking for. The long knee-length, the short bolero, and the mid-thigh length are all suitable choices depending on your body type and comfort level. A blazer that is more tailored at the waist area will usually be more flattering than a straight box. Thick shoulder pads will date most blazers. A natural slope is a better choice today. Are the sleeves too long? Hem them. If they are too short, hem them to three-quarter length. Remember, a blazer will feel more confining than a t-shirt or sweatshirt. Women will frequently pull their arms and shoulders in unnatural positions, showing just how tight the fabric feels. How often in your job do you reach above your head? A blazer two sizes too big creates a sloppy appearance. A properly fitting suit does feel different than a t-shirt and sweats, but with practice and a little time it will feel less strange and more natural.

Suits are blazers with pants and sometimes skirts. The fabrics and colors are the same between the pieces. I always recommend hanging them separately so you are reminded to use them in multiple ways. I have been questioned on this by some women in upper management—it is true that if one piece is dry cleaned more than the other, the fabric may fade differently. However, unless a woman has a job where she has to wear suits regularly, she will get a lot more wear out of the pieces by wearing them separately. Make the purchase work harder for you by wearing the pieces as much as possible.

Tops

These four types of tops will carry your outfits through many changes:

- Plain, no-pocket, solid-color t-shirts
- Solid-color tank tops
- Solid-color, short-sleeved shells
- Solid-color, tailored button-front blouses

The tailored button-front blouse can also be worn unbuttoned over another top to create a casual layered effect. You may want to remove the shoulder pads in your blouses if you frequently wear them under a jacket with shoulder pads. Velcro is great for offering the versatility of in-and-out shoulder pads. Shoulder pads have become much less noticeable. Some body types still look better with a bit of padding at the shoulder, but overall, the natural slope of the shoulder is a smart look.

Well-endowed women have more problems wearing button blouses because of the "gap" factor. A wonderful product called Hollywood Fashion Tape is basically a double-sided tape that can be put in place without fear of damaging the fabric. Velcro dots can be added to the gapping area also. A simple press joining the two sides should hold if there is not too much pressure to separate the two sides. It may be necessary to move up a size or two and then have the blouse tailored to fit better.

I suggest solid colors in the beginning to help you create that "classic style" look. Prints can range from very casual to very formal and are pieces you will want to add later. If you can find a simple print with your base color and the complementary color of your second blazer or pant, it will be worth the investment.

Accessories

Shoes in your base color, along with accessories, a handbag, trouser socks, or nylons will complete any outfit. I have a lot more to say on these topics in upcoming chapters.

Subtle Differences

Dressing appropriately for any situation is really the key to dressing successfully.

Try dressing up khakis or dark-colored jeans and a plain t-shirt by wearing a vest, adding a scarf, adding jewelry like a necklace or pin, tucking in the t-shirt and wearing a belt, or adding a cardigan, turtleneck, or blazer for another look.

Try dressing down a suit by separating pieces and adding a complementary color jacket or pant. Wear a plain, no-pocket t-shirt under the blazer and a casual shoe.

You may not need to wear a suit to work every day, but with just a few changes, a suit can offer all kinds of great looks:

*   More conservative—wear the suit with a silk or silk-like blouse. On a side note, the world of dress shoes has grown beyond the basic black pump. To keep it conservative, avoid open toes, glitter, and four-inch heels (unless you are very adapt at walking in them).
*   More relaxed—wear with a plain solid-color cotton shirt in a complementary color, and for an even more casual look, wear a striped t-shirt. Add a shoe with casual accents like a chain, tassels, etc.

- More casual—
  - pair the jacket with a light pair of khakis or dark jeans and a t-shirt or white cotton blouse.
  - wear the pants with a printed top and no jacket.
  - add a vest or cardigan.

Success Secret #6
How can you sell yourself if you don't think you have anything to sell? You are worth this opportunity.
Repeat this to yourself often.

Dressing for the Interview

Choose an outfit at least one or two steps above the job you are seeking. Keep it simple! If you are in doubt about what the company you are interviewing with considers appropriate interview attire, call and ask. I tell women to wear the outfit they intend to wear to the interview around the house first or out to a mall. Walk around. Get the feel of it. Is the outfit gapping or pulling? Practice sitting down as well as walking up and down stairs. It is better to discover that your blouse becomes too revealing when you move around a couple days prior to your interview rather than during the interview. Remember, you want to be able to concentrate on the interview and on answering the questions rather than obsessing about the fact that your skirt keeps sliding up to an uncomfortable length.

I realize many job applications are now taken over the Internet, but don't overlook local opportunities. If you go in to ask for an application or to return one, be prepared and dress for an interview. On occasion you may be asked to interview right then. At the very least the person taking your paperwork may be doing the interviews or may be asked to give his or her impression of you. Never take a friend along. ALWAYS be aware that while you are sitting and waiting for your interview, someone could be evaluating you. Avoid texting or talking on the phone.

Dressing for the Job

A woman from a bank-skills training program came into Ready for Success. She was uncertain whether she even wanted a blazer. We convinced her to try on a lovely Jones New York suit, just for fun. After seeing herself in the three-way mirror, she turned around to face us with the most amazed look on her face. "I really do look like a bank teller!" Until that moment, I don't think she saw herself mentally in the position she was training for. We laughed and said, "You look like a loan officer or even vice president of the bank!" And suddenly a world of opportunities opened before her eyes.

Diana Saiki of Ball State University has done some wonderful research on the importance of a professional appearance at work in her article, "Building Opportunities: Dressing for Success." Her research has shown that employees are more productive when dressed appropriately for their job.[1] Especially in the beginning, you want to feel confident and capable of doing your job.

Success Secret #7
Almost everyone who has ever accepted a job or promotion thinks, "This is over my head and sooner or later they will find out that I don't really know what I am doing." Never let fear stop you from taking on a new challenge.

You want to look responsible and capable of handling the job, especially in the mirror. So put your shoulders back and believe you can do it because in no time you will be doing it. I have discovered dressing the part goes along with acting the part to develop the con-

---

1   Diana Saiki. "Building Opportunities: Dressing for Success," The Forum for Family and Consumer Issues 10, no. 2 (2005), http://ncsu.edu/ffci/publications/2005/v10-n2-2005-october/pa-2-building.php.

fidence needed to fill the part. I have seen this with many women at *Ready for Success* as well as with myself.

Other employees may comment that you "over-dress," but that is usually because by your "dressing up" you have set a higher standard for everyone in the office. The only person you may not want to dress better than is the boss—unless you want her job.

daywear vs. datewear

Daywear Versus Datewear

I peered into the window at the bank drive-up. The young woman about to take my deposit tugged the thin strap of her top. She obviously was not wearing a bra. *"Well at least she had straps holding up her top this week. Last week it was only a tube top with no straps,"* I thought to myself. The bank teller made me a little nervous taking my deposit. She looked as though she needed the money more than I did.

Later that day, a tall, young, beautiful size 8 woman and I had just finished selecting her work wardrobe when we stepped into the final room for selections—the miscellaneous collection. This room is the "fun" stuff like shorts outfits and even gowns at holiday time. She grabbed a cute little black leather mini skirt off the rack. "This would be just perfect for the concert I am going to next week. I'll borrow my sister's leather boots. I am going to look so hot!"

I laughed and replied, "Great, but don't wear it to work!"

She stopped and with all seriousness said, "I know. I was sent home from work last week for wearing a mini skirt. No one ever told me not to wear a mini skirt to work; I see them do it on TV."

This woman learned a valuable lesson, but unfortunately it was the hard way.

Too Sexy

Dressing "too sexy" is the biggest mistake I see young women make who lack the experience of dressing for the workplace. Whether it's a skirt that's too tight, too short, or slit too high; a strappy little sandal with a four-inch heel; revealing tops; or lingerie as suggestive outwear, those outfits will get you noticed. But will it be the positive type of notice you desire for advancement?

Unfortunately, not all workplaces will honestly discuss what they expect their employees to wear. Some male supervisors feel very uncomfortable discussing a woman's suggestive attire with her. I admit part of the problem is the difference in body type. A low-cut top on a woman with small breasts will present much differently than a low-cut top on a well-endowed woman. You may see other employees dressing this way. In many cases, no one will comment directly to you about your similar clothing selection, but rest assured, someone is noticing. It may come up behind your back, during layoff reviews, or when being considered for advancement. Remember, you are representing your employer and company. An employer has the right to expect a certain appearance from employees. Women are frequently surprised when I mention this fact to them.

Success Secret #8

Dress for your workplace. You are representing your employer by how you dress and present yourself—not your eligibility on the dating circuit.

Datewear or Daywear?

Clothing Type	Datewear image	Daywear image
Blouses and tops	Very low cut, either scoop neck, V-neck, or unbuttoned to breast	No or very little cleavage exposure
	Too tight, gapping buttons	Proper size; mini-mizer bra if needed
	Animal prints, suggestive logos or slogans	Animal prints worn under blazer, just peeking out
	See-through	See-through with proper camisole or under-blouse
	Tube tops	May be worn as strapless bra under clothing
	Tank tops with spaghetti straps or built-in bra	May be worn under unbuttoned blouse or jacket, not too tight, no cleavage showing; or don't remove the jacket during work hours.
Skirts and dresses	Slit above the knee to mid-thigh or higher	Slit to knee
	Mini Skirt	No Shorter than the width of a credit card above the knee (the narrow width) when kneeling on the floor. Check the length by kneeling in front of a mirror.

Clothing Type	Datewear image	Daywear image
	Tight, every bulge and muscle shows	Try sitting down. Can you do it comfortably? Ask someone you trust to give you an honest opinion. How does it look from the back?
Accessories	Large earrings that dangle below your chin line	Simplify your accessory choices
Shoes	Open toes	See chapter on SHOES
	Glittering gold and silver colors	Basic neutral colors to match your outfit, preferably your pants or skirt
	4-inch heels or higher	3 inches or under
Make-up	Strong blush, bright lipsticks, heavy eye shadows, colored mascaras	Brown or black mascara, colors of lipstick leaning toward naturals tones
Hair	Dramatic hairstyles or long hair dyed un-natural colors	Clean, pulled away from face (especially if long) and always nicely trimmed

Some basic outfits, with a few modifications, can very easily take you from the office to an evening out. Changing from a two-inch black pump to a strappy black sandal, unbuttoning another button on your blouse to reveal your lacy camisole, rolling the waistband of your skirt from "office" length to "mini" length, adding a small evening purse, changing to fun glittery jewelry, and adding a bit more make-up can create a new look for an after-work date or event.

Love in the Workplace

A very good friend of mine has had a long career with a large, well-known corporation. She vowed in the very beginning of her career not to date anyone at work. She has had plenty of opportunity, but the negatives far outweigh the positives.

Many employers have rules against dating in the workplace. Experience has shown that when personal and emotional issues erupt in the workplace (as they sometimes do between two people who are dating), the whole work environment suffers. The issues that may arise if one of the employees is supervising another are even more catastrophic. So if you are dressing to impress a particular someone at work or seeking a possible mate from your workplace, think again. Dress to be seen as a confident, hardworking, responsible, capable employee for the people who give the promotions and the raises. Do your dating and mate selection outside the workplace.

If you are a single woman, think about the type of man you would like to attract. How you present yourself, even on the dating scene, sends signals you may or may not want to send. Where do you want to be in five or ten years, and with whom? Are you currently dating a caring, confident, capable, responsible person on the road to a successful life? Do you attract that type of person? If you don't, what can you do to change even your dating image? Change the way you dress!

CHAPTER FIVE

Accessories: Friend or Foe?

Even in a business casual world a few pieces of jewelry, a scarf, a color-coordinated outfit, and an appropriate looking polished shoe present the image that…
* you know what you are doing.
* you are confident in what you are doing.
* you care enough to make the effort to present yourself professionally.

Accessories can bring a simple pair of khakis and a plain t-shirt to a level that shows that you care what you look like. On the other side, accessories can be overdone and, instead of creating a classic appearance, you move into the realm of cartoonish exaggeration of a character from a bad sitcom. Remember to limit your accessories:
* A watch
* A pair of simple earrings
* A scarf OR necklace
* One or two rings
* Maybe a bracelet

Success Secret #9
Accessories can add the "WOW!" to a simple outfit, but overdoing accessories can create
the cartoonish appearance of a sitcom character!
Choose one focal point!

The Sisterhood of the "Secret Scarf Society"

Have you ever wandered by the scarf selection at a fine department store and wondered to yourself, who wears those things? Can I afford to buy them? Would I look good in one? I found my first scarf at a friend's garage sale. It was a large square scarf suitable for "shawling" over a coat or blazer. ("Shawling" I'll explain in a moment.) I took it home, hung it over a chair, and stared at it for weeks. Finally I gently folded it and put it in a drawer. Another month passed and I could almost hear it calling me every time I opened the drawer. Finally I took out my navy blazer, hung it over a chair, and dressed the jacket with the scarf as a shawl. That evening for a meeting at church, I put on the jacket and shawl. A friend approached and said, "Joyce, I love your scarf. I never know how to wear them but love to see them on people." Thus began my introduction as a sister of the "Secret Scarf Society" (SSS).

Success Secret #10
There is no real secret to wearing a scarf. Put it on.
Decide what feels comfortable to you. Then carry it off with attitude! No fussing or fidgeting allowed.

Occasionally someone will suggest a new way to tie a scarf. Don't take it as a negative comment about the way you have yours tied. These women usually just want to share and to let you know they too are sisters of the SSS.

A Suitable Start
The large wrap scarves and pashminas have become very popular. Pashmina is made from the underbelly wool of a mountain goat. The wool is very similar to cashmere. I like them best mixed with silk, 70% pashmina/cashmere and 30% silk. These scarves are very long wearing because of the natural fibers. If they scratch your

chin they are probably made of another wool blend no matter how they are marked. Pashmina-feel and pashmina-acrylic are all man-made fibers and should be priced less expensively. Pashminas are a great way to start wearing scarves. They can be…

- wrapped around your neck once and flipped over your shoulder.
- doubled length-wise then doubled width-wise and laid across your shoulders with the loose ends pulled through the created loop.
- repeated as above, only threaded one end over and one under to create a braided look.
- with a scarf in front of the neck, wrapped behind and back to front, either with the ends hanging down or tied in front.
- doubled length-wise with the folded side facing away from your throat, the ends wrapped around behind your neck and then brought back to the front. This will create a loop in front of your throat. Now wrap the long ends through the loop once or twice. Leave the fringe hanging out beneath the wrapped loop. You can tighten it up close to your neck or pull it away more to create a cowl effect.
- worn as a shawl wrapped gently around your shoulders on a cool evening.

Scarves come in a multitude of fabrics, colors, patterns, and shapes to help any woman find at least one that adds that special signature of style to her wardrobe. I love silk scarves. I now own over a hundred scarves. Okay, I know that is a bit excessive. I have a hard time resisting the gorgeous colors and choices of how to wear them. **WARNING: COLLECTING SCARVES CAN BE ADDICTIVE!** Scarves can take the simplest outfit from bland to impressive with just the twist of a knot.

The scarves in neutrals, black, white, gray, and navy can add extra pizzazz to the simplest outfit. Try bright jewel tones with the neutrals—black, navy, or gray. Try soft pastels with the more muted neutrals in your closet.

I still find scarves at yard sales, estate sales, consignment shops, and thrift shops where frequently they are carefully folded and still in the box. I suspect they were purchased on a whim and then put in the drawer, haunting the purchaser until, in a fit of frustration, they were given away.

I have included illustrations of several simple ties. More ideas can be found in scarf-tying tip pamphlets lying in dresser drawers all over America! This is one of those areas in which you can spend hours on the Internet shopping for scarves and finding new ways to tie them. Move them out of the drawers and closets. Put them on, ladies!

Okay, I Have a Scarf. Now What Do I do With It?
Here are several simple ties to begin experimenting with.

Long lapel scarves can be...

- easily laid under the lapel of a jacket or blazer for the beginner.
- tied in front in a simple square knot or overhand knot.
- doubled and with the ends pulled through the created loop.
- wrapped around the neck twice and tied in a simple knot.
- tied as a man's four-in-hand tie (see Chapter 12).
- tied in a simple overhand knot on one side with the other side pulled through the knot.
- knotted together at the ends, creating a loop, then looped around your neck twice. This is the duplicate of the infinity scarf.

Large square scarves can be...

- folded into a triangle and "shawled" over a top or jacket, either left to hang down or tied in a knot in front or to the side.

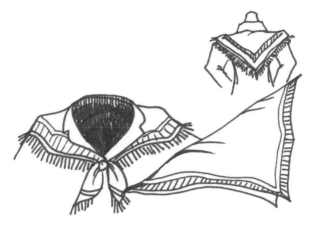

- folded into a triangle and worn under a jacket as a blouse effect.
- used to create a long, lapel-like shape if you fold two sides into the center.

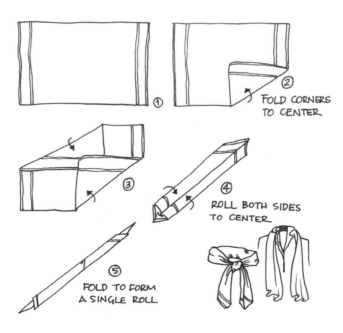

① ② FOLD CORNERS TO CENTER

③ ④ ROLL BOTH SIDES TO CENTER

⑤ FOLD TO FORM A SINGLE ROLL

Small square scarves can be...

- folded into the center creating a long ribbon to wrap around your neck, with the knot placed in front or off to one side.
- folded into the center and knotted in the middle with the knot placed in the middle of your throat and the ends tied in back of your neck, creating a necklace effect.

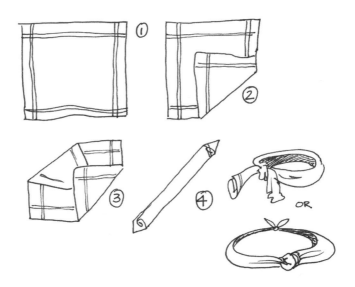

Fabrics

One hundred percent silk or soie scarves are generally hand rolled along the edge. Usually the colors are brighter on the top side. They can have a variety of different feels, all of them very nice to the touch. Silk scarves will frequently say "dry clean only." I have had success with washing them by hand in cold water with a gentle detergent or dish soap, rolling them up in a towel to remove moisture, and then ironing them on the "silk" setting while still damp. Be sure to use a cotton fabric between the iron and the fabric. The pressing cloth protects the delicate fabric from the heat and occasional dirty iron. I find I very seldom need to wash them unless they accidentally serve as my bib during a meal. I have had two vintage scarves "bleed" colors with this method, so beware. This method also works for pashminas. Steaming also works to restore a badly wrinkled scarf to its original elegance.

Wool scarves can come in a variety of weights, from a summer weight to a heavy weight suitable for "shawling" over a coat in the winter. Wool can cause some people to itch, so be sure and do the chin test before buying.

Rayon and polyester scarves are made all over the world, come in lovely colors, and can be just as soft and delicate to the touch as silk. They are usually machine stitched along the edge. I do find some polyester scarves will have a slightly scratchy feel.

If you are concerned the scarf will slip around on you, hold it in place with a pierced earring hidden in the fold of the fabric. You can also purchase special little pins for this. I find them frequently at garage sales and thrift shops.

Organizing Scarves

I like to hang long lapel scarves from a plastic hanger with round holes especially designed for this purpose. I keep the hanger on a hook in my bedroom near my mirror. Not only does the rack of scarves look pretty, but also they are close by and not easily overlooked while I am dressing in the morning. I have used a foam-covered (the foam prevents the scarves from easily slipping off) wire hanger to hang scarves, and even a standing quilt rack will work.

And, yes, they can be neatly folded and kept in a drawer, but you might be apt to wear them more frequently if they are kept in view. To avoid creases, you can wrap them around empty paper cylinders from paper towels or even toilet paper.

Jewelry: Classy or Trashy?

Watches

Today so many of us depend on our cell phones for the time that fewer of us are wearing watches. But watches are a recommended piece of jewelry. I have been told by *Ready for Success* volunteers who work in human resources departments that wearing a watch indicates to an interviewer that you are concerned about time. Time equals money in the business world. Will you be concerned enough about time to get to your desk when you are expected or be concerned about deadlines? Just wearing a watch can start those questions off on the right track. Of course the trick is to be sure and show up on time for the interview—15 minutes early is your goal.

Watches come in some very nice gold and silver combinations, allowing you to match both types of jewelry with one. Some women have told me they are allergic to the base metal many watches are made of. This allergy is usually to nickel, so look for a quality watch with a stainless steel back. A leather strap watchband is sometimes a better choice if your skin is sensitive. Applying clear nail polish to the exposed metal will help some people with metal allergies. Or wear the watch bracelet-style so it doesn't sit too tightly against the skin. This may prevent a reaction from developing.

Earrings

If you wear earrings, only wear two earrings to an interview—one in each ear. In other words, avoid multiple earrings. Keep the earrings you choose simple. Refrain from wearing those that dangle below the chin line. Earrings should be one inch or less in length. This is an area I advise new employees to watch for a while. Get to know your employer before showing up with big dangling earrings and multiple piercings. If the first comment you get is, "Nice earrings," with a slight edge of sarcasm, save those earrings for datewear.

Necklaces

The rule with necklaces is, once again, keep it simple. Interesting necklaces are acceptable in the workplace but can be very distracting if they make a lot of noise as you walk or overpower your clothing. If the print on your top is bold, keep the accessories quiet. Bolder necklaces are carried off better against a quieter, solid background.

Bracelets

When you first start a new job, limit how many bracelets you wear to one or two. If your job requires a lot of keyboarding, avoid clanging or rattling bracelets altogether. The noise can be very disturbing to people around you.

Brooches or Pins

Brooches and pins are items of jewelry that can really allow your individual interests to come alive and create conversation starters at a new job. If you choose an interesting brooch or pin, limit your other jewelry to simple earrings and maybe a plain necklace. Pins can be found in your grandmother's jewelry box or maybe in your own that you've not looked in for a long time. You can even make them from large outdated earrings by popping off the clip or post and gluing on a pin back. Brooches, pins, and even earrings that would make interesting pieces can frequently be found at consignment shops, garage sales, and clearance sales.

Handbags: Size Does Matter

Handbags are no longer required to match your belt and shoes. Choosing a handbag in a size that fits your needs in your base wardrobe color is sensible in the beginning. Some women still change purses daily to match their outfits, but more and more women today use just one or two bags. Changing purses daily is just too time consuming. Collecting your make-up in one small bag and other small items in another does make changing purses easier. Move the two or three already organized bags into another handbag and go. If finding your credit cards in your purse is a problem, I listed a product called Trendy Tabs in the Resources section of this book. These handy little tabs attach to the edge of your credit cards to make finding them easier—a great idea by a couple of women entrepreneurs filling a need.

I do suggest taking a small handbag to an interview, unless you take a briefcase, and then don't take a handbag at all. A large overflowing handbag at an interview gives the impression of disorganization. Remember it is about the impression. If you can fit a small notebook, your keys, identification (especially your social security card, which may be required for a job application), a small amount of money, a debit card or checkbook, a written list of references, and a pen into your purse, that should be all you need. Always bring a copy of your resume. It may only be available in a digital format, and the day of your interview the computers are down. It may have been misfiled. Be prepared with an extra copy in a folder.

I tend to carry too large a bag daily, but I frequently will have a smaller bag in my car to put just the essentials in if I want to make a better impression. Unload your purse. Are there things you can do without? This is my biggest mistake. I always seem to think I need everything in there, but then I wind up fumbling through the collection to find what I am looking for and creating the dreaded image of disorganization.

To Belt or Not to Belt?

Wear a belt if your pants have belt loops. I suggest avoiding contrasting colors of belts if you and your waist are happier without the emphasis. If you are short-waisted, a belt to match your top will give the appearance of added length. If you are long-waisted, match the belt to your pants to shorten up the appearance of your torso and lengthen your legs. Wide, low-slung belts with short crop tops exposing the belly button fall into the datewear category. If you don't have a belt to match your pants, tuck in your top and blouse it over the exposed loops slightly. This is a better choice than the totally wrong belt. Many tops are now designed to be untucked if they have a straight edge and are not so long as to look sloppy.

Shoes deserve their very own chapter
... and they shall have one!

CHAPTER SIX

Shoes Are Not Thine Enemy!

Your shoes make a statement when you enter the room, especially when you're at work. Tottering in on four-inch heels you are unaccustomed to wearing gives the impression you dressed up from your mother's closet. The other end of the spectrum is arriving in badly worn shoes or tennis shoes (even colored ones). Putting on a pair of running shoes for a walk at lunch, or wearing them to or from the car or public transit is acceptable, but change to a basic shoe when you're in the office.

Shoes can come in fun fashion statements, but keep in mind the basic rule of many work places: no open-toed shoes. The exposure of your toes, even with a lovely pedicure and nail polish, diminishes the authority you might command when you walk into the room. Women might comment on your cute shoes or even the color of your nail polish. Men tend to see it as a frivolous thing in which women indulge themselves. Do you want to be seen in the workplace as frivolous? It will not command the respect and positive attention you should be seeking from your employer. There is a current trend to wear a cute strappy little sandal with a business suit in the summer. I suggest you follow this trend in your workplace only if the owner or president of the company does. Otherwise throw such shoes into a bag and wear them out to dinner. Remember, what is the image you want to project? Are cute strappy little sandals projecting power, authority, and professionalism?

Begin building your shoe wardrobe with a quality pump with a two-inch heel or less in basic black. If the shoe is really comfortable for you and a good fit for your foot and budget, buy two pairs. As your budget allows, add shoes with white stitching, buckles, tassels, and multi-tones, as well as boots. Those extra shoe selections become ones you add as you find a dependable source for your shoes or a very reasonable shoe sale. Many fine department stores will have shoe clearance rooms and regular sales in quality shoes.

Remember when buying off the sale rack, the right shoe has probably been tried on several times. If it is real leather it will have stretched and feel very comfortable. My left foot is about a half size larger than my right, so before purchasing shoes, I always need to try on both shoes, expecting the left to be slightly tighter. Leather shoes will stretch with use, so my question when trying on shoes is, will the left become as comfortable as the right? If you have a really distinct difference in your foot size, fit the larger foot and pad the shoe that is smaller with tissue in the toe, or use specially designed heel inserts. I also determine what weight of sock or nylon I will be wearing with the shoe. With my basic shoe for work, I wear either nylons or trouser socks—never heavy cotton socks. Wearing heavier socks will stretch out leather shoes, and they will feel too big or sloppy the next time I wear nylons or trouser socks with them. If they are tennis shoes or very casual shoes that I expect to wear with heavy socks, then I keep a pair of those socks tucked in the shoes for that walk at lunch.

I don't care how cute the shoes are or how good the deal is, I don't buy them if they are too big or too small. Wearing shoes too big causes you to shuffle when you walk. Shoes that are too small (besides the obvious pain) over time cause problems for the feet that will then limit your shoe choices even more.

Remember, no shoes are a great deal if they sit in your closet unworn. Even the finest shoe manufacturer can make some ugly, uncomfortable shoes.

Shoes purchased for the workplace…

- should be comfortable to wear for at least eight to ten hours.
- should be classic in design.
- should match a multitude of outfits.
- should present a professional appearance.

Caring for Your Shoe Investment

Shoetrees are a good addition to your closet wardrobe. Shoetrees are plastic, metal, or wood; are adjustable in size; and fit in your shoes to help them hold their shape. I have found fitting shoetrees into a new of pair of shoes allows them to stretch slightly and will improve their wearability. If the shoes need just a little stretching, now is the time to wear them around the house wearing heavy cotton socks. They should feel much better the next time you wear them with trouser socks or nylons. Stuffing them with newspaper very tightly until the next time you wear them will also help stretch out a pair of leather shoes.

Keeping your shoes on racks in your closet allows you to see and quickly select shoes appropriate for your outfit. Shoe racks are also available to hang on the back of your door. I have never had enough closet space, but one woman I know keeps each pair of shoes in the original box with a snapshot stapled to the end of the box for easy viewing. Some women use the clear shoeboxes available from discount stores or closet stores with the same idea of protecting the shoes while allowing for easier selection. I do suggest leaving shoes sit out in the open for about 24 hours after wearing them to allow them a reasonable airing out. Shoes will last longer if you can rotate their use frequently.

Success Secret #12

Shoes last longer if you polish them regularly and rotate their use! Well-tended shoes say a lot about your attention to detail and concern about your appearance.

Gretchen, one of the *Ready for Success* volunteers who works with clothing, happened by as a woman and her personal shopper were making a shoe selection. The woman had selected a nice black leather shoe. Gretchen, noticing the shoes needed polishing, took them in the backroom and polished them. The woman smiled, as her shoes now looked new. A couple of months later she returned for her second visit, and upon seeing Gretchen, kicked off her shoes and said, "Can you polish my shoes again?" Gretchen laughed, "I'll be happy to show you how to polish them yourself!"

There are many products that allow you to polish different colors of shoes with the same clear leather protection. These can be purchased from quality shoe stores, shoe repair shops, or online. They are expensive, but my experience of quickly polishing six pairs of shoes and the resulting improvement in appearance has made the investment worthwhile. The products also tend to last a long time. These products work well on the fine leather purse or leather jacket you may have found at a garage sale or estate sale in need of a little attention. I like Doc Marten's Wonder Balsam. It also protects from water damage. Do not use it on suede or patent leather.

Traditional shoe polish also comes in small round jars of crème, small tins of harder wax consistency, and bottles. Each of these is a predetermined color to use on a special color of shoe. I suggest brushing the dirt off the shoe, applying a thin layer of polish with a soft rag, allowing it to dry, wiping it with another clean rag, and finishing with a rapid buffing using a shoe brush or soft clean rag. I have found little difference other than in the application between the three types of colored polishes.

Synthetic, not leather, shoes can be cleaned using a little window spray cleaner or any other household spray cleaner. Patent leather shoes clean up the best using a small amount of petroleum jelly rubbed into the surface. Suede or fabric shoes are best brushed with a soft brush to remove dirt and stains.

Shoe repair shops are becoming harder and harder to find and usually are expensive. If you tend to wear out your heels quickly or need a slight stitch repair, I would suggest an estimate first. If you find a good quality shoe repair with reasonable prices, let me know. I'm always seeking the quality workmanship that is difficult to find today.

Consider good quality shoes a worthwhile investment. If you live in a part of the country where it rains or snows frequently, consider wearing boots to work and changing once you arrive at the office. Watermarks and salt stains can be removed from leather shoes but rarely from fabric. If you have shoetrees, put them in wet shoes to retain their shape while drying, or simply stuff wet shoes with newspaper. Do not put them directly near a heat source, as drying too quickly can permanently damage leather.

Shoes protect your feet. Their appearance says something about your attention to detail and can project a negative image when they are too casual, too fancy, too dirty, or too damaged. So, when you are dressing for an interview or for a job, don't forget your feet!

CHAPTER SEVEN

Keeping Up Appearances

Employers and co-workers are willing to forgive and learn to overlook many things about the way you present yourself, as long as your presentation is clean and your work ethic is sterling. But I cannot emphasis enough how important it is that when you go in for the interview and every day of work, you take the time to prepare yourself. The details create an image of organization and care for your appearance and, thus, for your job and employer. Remember you are representing not only your employer but also yourself.

Success Secret #13
The details matter! Whether you work in a professional setting or a more casual setting, the details of your personal appearance are important.

Your Hands

Are your nails trimmed and even? They don't have to be long and perfect. In fact, if you are applying for a position that requires a lot of keyboarding, long nails sometimes give the impression they will interfere with your job performance. (Remember, I said "the impression." Grow them back once you have the job and have had the opportunity to prove they don't interfere with your job performance.) If you are trying to enter the medical field, I would not recommend artificial nails. The concerns that arose from trapped bacteria several years ago still make some people nervous. Carry a small emery board or nail file to repair those last minute nicks and tears. Filing their nails regularly has helped some women overcome the nail-biting habit. Keep a cuticle oil or crème near your sink or in your purse; a quick rub into those cuticles will help keep them looking good.

Are your nails clean? If you like to do a lot of gardening, wear garden gloves. Wear gloves when painting or working with harsh cleaning materials or chemicals around the house. Keep a nailbrush near your bathroom sink and use it.

Nail polish? Keep to simple, natural colors, although some shades might be acceptable such as reds, deep pinks, or oranges. Definitely avoid purple, green, black, and blue. I realize dark unnatural colors are very popular, but remember your interviewer, your work colleagues, or your customers may view your nail color choice more negatively than your peers do. If your nail polish is chipped, remove it all.

Keep in mind you will be shaking hands with many people, especially while interviewing. Use a little light lotion if you have dry hands, but not as you walk in the door of the interview. Use it earlier to allow time for it to absorb. Arid climates, too much time in heated buildings in the winter, washing dishes, and excessive hand washing can all lead to dry, scaly skin. Plan ahead—use a sugar scrub (2–3 times a week), cuticle oil or cream, and lotion daily to keep your hands in better shape. I use Nana's Homemade Sugar Scrub recipe.

Nana's Homemade Sugar Scrub

- One cup sugar. (I like using raw sugar, but superfine can be found in most baking aisles.)
- 1/2 cup olive oil or less. (Almond, coconut, and palm oils work too.)
- One tablespoon of honey.
- One teaspoon of vanilla. (Use real vanilla; seek out non-alcoholic varieties. I have one that uses glycerin as its base agent. Beware that alcohol is a drying agent. I have found putting vanilla beans in sugar and adding this sugar instead of the liquid vanilla works very well.)
- Option A: Add a bit of vitamin E by either opening a couple of capsules or buying a small bottle and using a few drops at a time.
- Option B: Salt (I like kosher salt, grain size) can be used instead of the sugar, but it is painful if you have cracked hands. I like the salt scrub for my feet and heels, especially after using a pumice stone.
- I keep the sugar scrub next to my sink. I use it enough I have not had problems with it turning bad. You can find other recipes and suggestions on the Internet. I have not been happy with the brown sugar suggestions.
- I find sugar scrub too harsh for the sensitive skin on my face.

The exfoliation of the sugar scrub removes the dry, dead skin and allows your skin to be more receptive to lotion. There are many wonderful options for lotion. Check the Resources section to find some of my favorites.

Most of us have problems with our palms sweating when we get nervous, so you probably do not need a heavy lotion. If you have very sweaty palms, carry a tissue or dry washcloth to use prior to going into the interview.

It has only been recently that we have begun to teach our daughters to shake hands as we do our sons. I remember early in *Ready for Success*'s development, a very good male friend and supporter pulled me aside and said, "Joyce, you need to learn how to shake hands." I was expected to meet and greet people while representing *Ready for Success*, but I would get nervous with every handshake. Was I doing it right? Would they know I did not know what I was doing? I would look down or away, avoiding eye contact. Practice has improved that handshake. Now I shake hands with confidence, including my daughters' friends' hands, to their surprise.

Shaking Hands

- Always stand to shake hands.
- Extend your right hand, grasping the right hand of the recipient of your handshake, web to web. Hold your wrist taut. Shake with your lower arm, not your hand.
- The grasp should be firm but not smashing.
- Look the person whose hand you are shaking in the eye and SMILE.
- Greet and exchange names.
- One or two pumps of the arm is sufficient.
- Relax your grip to release.
- It is acceptable to cover your right hand slightly with your left, as a show of warmth or affection.

During the handshake is a good time to repeat your name and that of the person you are meeting. Physical touch helps to imprint names in your memory.

Always wear your name badge on the right shoulder. During the handshake, your name will be more easily visible and, again, memorable.

Your Hair

Clean hair is very important. Your hair frames your face and adds to or detracts quickly from that first impression. Keep your hair clean. If you don't, it will be one of the first things noticed.

If you have long hair, pulling it back will add to the professional appearance. Several years ago there was a commercial advertising shampoo. The woman, you may remember, untied her hair on the way out of the office to meet her friends at a restaurant. That is datewear versus daywear, once again.

A good professional haircut can help solve many hair problems. Search out a salon that teaches hair cutting and styling. Usually the prices are cheaper, as the students learn on you. They are watched over by professional, experienced stylist, so it can be worth the "risk." I have used such beauty or cosmetology schools. I once found a young student I liked so much I followed her to her first place of employment and eventually her own business.

If you are into wildly colored or spiked hair, you might consider one of the rinse-out colors for your weekend fun. Remember, you are representing your employer, and what the wild colors say about you may not be what your employer wants your hair to say about the business.

Your Body

Regular bathing does not mean just once a week or on Saturday night. Avoid heavy perfumed scents. Soap and water daily will do the trick.

Many workplaces have become sensitive to scent allergies in employees. Save your special colognes and perfumes for your social life, not the workplace.

The lack of, or failure of, deodorant is a topic that can be sensitive to discuss with even your closest friends. Americans spend huge sums of money to cover, disguise, and hide their body odors. You might ask someone close to you if they recommend a particular brand of deodorant as you are considering a brand change. A quick, positive response will tell you to begin seeking stronger odor protection.

Even baking soda patted on the underarms can help control body odor. Small packets of baby wipes can be very useful for quick cleanups. They come in many pleasing scents and even unscented. Strong, offensive body odors can signal ill health.

Your Face

Another delicate topic is facial hair removal. In this country we find excessive hair on a woman's face very distracting. There are a number of products available for hair removal: depilatories, waxing, sugaring, tweezing, threading, electrolysis, shaving, lasers, and a few new topical creams different from depilatories. Most of them have to be tested to see what works for your skin type. Many can cause rashes, skin bumps, and even burns. I will admit that once you begin removing the hair on your chin or upper lip, it will be ongoing except possibly if you use laser treatment (the most expensive). Excessive hair growth on women can be related to medical conditions. A visit with your primary physician may be in order before beginning any removal process. Bleaching facial hair is another option that needs to be repeated every few weeks or months. This does not remove the hair or change the texture. It only lightens what hair there is. Damage to the skin is still possible with this method.

Easy on the make-up!

- Use mascara in black or brown, and avoid colors, especially for the interview.
- Eyeliner should simply accent the eyes during the day.
- Eye shadow often isn't even necessary in the day. Save dramatic colors and patterns for your evenings out.
- Lipstick in a natural color (in other words no black, cherry red, bright frosted pink, etc.) should be enough.
- Foundation (if worn) should be natural looking.
- Blush (if worn) should be simple with daywear but can be more dramatic with eveningwear.

Your Smile

Your smile matters! If your teeth are in need of repair, you might search out a medical school that teaches dentistry. These schools frequently offer reduced rates. You become a subject for the student to work on but under the watchful eye of a more experienced and usually able dentist. You might also search out a private dentist who will allow you to pay your bill in monthly installments.

Teeth whitening has become expected. The cost can be as simple as upgrading your toothpaste to a whitening one or as expensive as laser treatments. More options are now available over-the-counter and no longer require a dental visit or multiple dental visits.

Brush your teeth! Floss too. And brush your tongue. Doing this every morning and evening will improve your smile and breath. Bad breath can be a sign of tooth decay, sinus infection, and other health issues. See your doctor if regular dental hygiene does not clear up your breath.

Have you tried the Neti pot, or sinus rinse, method? This can be very effective for allergy sufferers. It feels quite strange to do the rinse in the beginning, but it is very effective for chronic nasal drainage.

Show me a woman with a smile on her face and eyes that reflect the knowledge that she looks good, and I'll show you a beautiful woman!

Your Body Piercings

I recommend just one earring in each ear lobe at interviews. Before wearing multiple ear piercings to work, let your coworkers get to know you. Save the multiples for datewear or social events.

Jewelry for facial piercings is best removed for the interview process. Some employers have strict policies concerning facial piercings. Follow the policy of the employer after being hired. Tongue piercings, in particular, can affect your speech. Effective and clear communication is important in the interview and on the job. I have known people with tongue piercings who insist it does not affect their speech. They then sit there and roll the piercing around in their mouth. That is more distracting than chewing gum.

Other body piercing, such as a belly button piercing, is something your coworkers need never know about. You should never reveal your belly button in the workplace anyway! That goes for other body piercings also.

See Chapter 12 for my thoughts on gauging.

Your Tattoos

I have worked with many young women who regret the tattoos

on their hands, wrists, arms, and ankles because of the past lifestyle they now represent. Even what was considered a cute little pair of feet on the ankle in high school or college now causes them to reconsider a skirt for an interview. They frequently choose long sleeves to cover arm and wrist tattoos. Covering the tattoos on the hands is the most difficult. Make-up or actual removal may be necessary. If your tattoos represent a lifestyle you now hope to move beyond, see if there is an organization that supports and promotes tattoo removal. While tattoos have become more socially acceptable, even fun ones can send a message in our society due to the possible connection to gangs and violence. Corporate and conservative employers seldom find them acceptable.

Success Secret #16
If you get a tattoo, never put it where it can be seen in an interview.

Your Lingerie
Lingerie is meant to be worn UNDER clothing, not as outerwear, despite what fashion magazines may tell you. We meet women almost daily at *Ready for Success* in need of undergarments. Properly fitting undergarments are more comfortable and provide support under your clothing to present a more appropriate appearance. Here are a few thoughts on lingerie for a working wardrobe:

- How deeply is your panty cutting into you and where? Are you revealing the type of underwear you have on? Pants or skirts that are too tight will more easily reveal a panty line.
- Brightly colored or dark-colored panties worn under light-colored pants and skirts will reveal themselves. So will wildly colored prints. Is that the image you want to portray? Are you revealing the type of underwear you have on?
- Brightly colored, dark, or wildly patterned bras will show through light-colored tops and blouses. These styles are for datewear, not daywear.

- If you have a difficult time with your upper thighs rubbing together and causing chaffing, try a panty shaped like a small short. The style is popular now and can even be found in the women's department. Male boxer shorts may also work for you. Who would know?
- Flesh-colored or champagne-colored bras are a good choice under white blouses. This will depend on your skin tone.
- Padded bras are sometimes referred to as "modesty bras." The padding helps disguise the protruding nipple.
- Wear the right size bra. The industry estimates 70% of women are wearing the wrong size bra. Bra manufacturers regularly send representatives out to fine department stores to measure women for the proper fit. These events are usually free to the public. Of course they are hoping to convince you to buy a bra, but this information can be extremely helpful the next time you are searching the discount racks.

A Properly Fitting Bra

Measure under your breasts around your rib cage, and add two inches if your measurement is an even number, or three inches if it is an odd number. This should give you the number dimension (32, 34, 36, 38, 40, 42, etc.) for your bra size. Bras are measured in even numbers. If you are between a number, remember the rule of rounding up: less than one-half inch, move down; one-half inch or more, move up. Wearing your best fitting non-padded cup, measure around the fullest part of your breast. If the measurement is one inch more than your earlier measurement, you are an A cup; two inches a B cup; three inches, a C cup; etc. The biggest mistake I see women making at *Ready for Success* is wearing a bra too small or not pulling their straps up firmly to provide the antigravity support most of us need. Bras do come in 48DD and 54F. They are just harder to find and more expensive. Extended sizes can be special ordered at the lingerie counter of most fine department stores. Less expensive resources might be found online or in catalogues or specialty shops. Your bra should hook on the middle row of hooks. Gained a little weight? Bra extenders can be purchased in most fabric stores. They simply add another one to two inches by connecting onto the existing hook system.

- Don't forget your bra size will go up and down as your weight changes.
- Camisoles are a great addition to a lingerie wardrobe. They can…
    - add cover to a colored bra.
    - provide warmth under a light blouse.
    - prevent a scratchy sweater from annoying you.
    - provide a more modest look under a thin blouse.

Camisoles can even have built-in bras. These are best for smaller breasted women.

Putting on Your Bra

Hook your bra in the back, lean over, and use your hand to sweep the breast tissue up and into the bra cup, first one side then the other. I was taught to hook my bra in the front and move it around to the back. This method is very hard on the band of the bra, causing it to wear out sooner. Stand and check to be sure…

- your straps are secure but not cutting into your shoulders.
- the front of your bra is lying flat against your chest and not poking out between your breasts.

Use the clips to adjust the length of your straps, bringing "the girls" up. If protruding nipples are a problem, several companies create silicon petals to place over your nipples under the bra.

Care Tips

Wash bras and camisoles in the gentle cycle in the washing machine or by hand. I always hook the hooks and place my bras in a mesh lingerie bag (available in many stores and online) when washing them in the machine. Use the hooks you don't normally hook when wearing the bra. They will stay connected better during the wash cycle. Without the lingerie bag, the hooks can become entangled with other articles of clothing.

Adding a half-cup of white vinegar to the wash will help remove perspiration stains.

Line-dry your bras so they last longer. Most bras contain spandex, which is slowly destroyed by the heat of a dryer. I have a towel rack hanging above my washer to place my bras on as they come out of the gentle cycle; of course there is always the shower curtain rod too.

After wearing a bra allow it to hang from a doorknob overnight to air out. This will extend the life of the spandex. Frequent washing shortens the lifetime of the material, as will wearing the same bra day after day. Have several bras to rotate in your closet.

Bras that are not underwire and have a narrow divider between cups can be twisted so one cup fits inside another and stored in a drawer.

Panties

Like all lingerie, panties are a very personal choice. I laughed when I read an ad saying if your panties peek above your waistline of your low-rider jeans be sure they are worth looking at. Your panties should NEVER show at work and that includes the "whale tail" (the top of thong underwear when the wearer bends over in low-rider pants). On the other side, your "granny panties" should not be so high that they roll over the waistband of your pants. Nevertheless, those two extremes leave a lot of room for personal choice in between.

Beyond Bras and Panties.

Wonderful products made of lightweight materials, most of them using spandex, are now available to complete your undergarment collection. These are NOT our grandmother's girdles. They come in a wide variety of shapes and coverage to help smooth the lumps and bumps of a woman's body. If items like this make you feel more polished and confident, check them out. They can be very expensive. To be honest, when you are just starting to build a wardrobe, this money may be better invested in leather shoes or a nice purse. Care for these garments just like you would a bra.

Panty Hose, Tights, Trouser Socks

As far as panty hose, tights, and trouser socks are concerned, I suggest dark pairs in the winter that match your shoes and skirts, creating a long line. I like lighter ones in natural colors in the summer so they match my skirt; I wear them with lighter shoes. If I am wearing a black skirt in the summer, I will choose off-black panty hose or a natural color with black shoes.

Many women select one size larger in panty hose for extra comfort. Buying multiple pairs of panty hose in the same color can save you money; if you get a run in one leg, save the pair of panty hose until you get a run in one leg of another matching pair. Then clip off the legs with runs about thigh high and slip on one pair and then the other. You will be wearing double panty tops (better tummy control), but each leg will be covered without a run. Many offices no longer require employees to wear nylons. Bare legs in the summer have become more acceptable. I have made my feelings clear about open-toed sandals, but if your workplace allows them and you still must wear nylons, avoid reinforced toe panty hose. Select what are called sandal-foot, or better yet, toeless, nylons.

Tights are a good choice under skirts and dresses in colder climates. They can come in interesting patterns, just like panty hose. You must decide how obvious of a statement you want to make by your choice of skirt or dress with them.

Buy trouser socks on sale. Trouser socks are thin nylon-like knee-highs that work wonderfully under slacks and even long skirts. They give a nice line to your ankle, are not too heavy in your shoe, and create a more polished look than bare legs or natural colored nylon. They come in extended sizes for women with heavier legs or larger feet.

Care for panty hose, tights, and trouser socks the same way you care for your bras. To keep them lasting longer, wash them in the gentle cycle in a mesh laundry bag, and hang them to dry. After they are dry, I will loosely tie my trouser socks in pairs to store in my drawer.

Caring for Your Clothing
Remember, this is your work uniform. Take care of it and it will last longer and serve you well. Whether buying from clearance racks, thrift stores, or wherever, you will have a considerable investment in your clothing, not only in dollars but also in working toward a better future. Here are some tips for getting the most out of your investment:

- Change clothes as soon as you come home. Now is the time to wear your jeans and t-shirts with cute logos.
- Hang up anything that is wearable for another day: the blazer, possibly the pants, and certainly anything that is dry clean only. Don't move them directly to the closet. Hang them from the shower rod or on a hook outside your closet to allow them to air out for 24 hours. I added an over-the-door rack to my bedroom door to air out clothing on.
- Place tops, trouser socks, etc. directly in the laundry pile, noting any spots in need of pretreatment. Painter's tape works well to mark a spot for spot removal before washing. Just don't leave the tape on for over a week.
- Slip into your fun shoes and let your work shoes air out.
- If the bottoms of your pants are becoming exceptionally frayed and dirty, you are wearing them too long!

Laundering Tips

- Separate your lights and your darks.
- Learn to use an iron. Check the Internet for some great videos. Use a clean cotton cloth between your iron and your light-colored and/or delicate clothing.
- Try one of the new wrinkle release products. Some people find it especially helpful on khakis.
- Remember to remove clothing promptly from the dryer before it cools off and the wrinkles are set. Over-drying clothing will also

set wrinkles in some synthetic fabrics. If you have forgotten to remove the clothing in a timely manner, a quick fluff on "no heat" may help, or throw in a damp towel and re-dry on low. Shake the clothing after removing it from the dryer before pulling it on a hanger. This will also help to remove wrinkles.

- If your water is rusty, add a rust remover product to the wash water, especially with your lighter colors.
- If you use public washers and dryers, search the insides for nasty surprises left behind before you put in your clothing. Run your hand around the inside searching for dyes, gum, or tar.
- Empty all pockets before washing clothing. An uncapped ink pen from my husband's pocket has damaged a couple of my shirts and blouses.
- Blazers and jackets are difficult to iron. Hang them in the bathroom while showering and the steam will usually help remove the wrinkles. Or use a steamer.
- Shoulder pads are less popular now than in the past, but many women with sloped shoulders like the balance they create with the rest of their body. Remove the shoulder pads from most blouses and tops before washing them. They will stay flat and create a smoother look longer. Use Velcro to reattach them.

The best action for stains is immediate reaction. At the very least, apply water to the stain. If you have a detergent pen in your purse or at your desk, use it. A paste of baking soda OR white vinegar on a swab can be very effective as a stain remover.

Dry Cleaning

There are some very good products out there for "dry clean only" clothing to use in your home dryer. I have found them most useful for odor removal and freshening. If you must have clothes cleaned professionally,

- check to see if there are self-serve dry cleaners in your area, or
- look for dry cleaning coupons and advertised specials.

Spots on clothes labeled "dry clean only" are still best removed by the dry cleaner. When you take in dry cleaning, be sure to point out the spot and, if possible, name the culprit. I had a lovely silk blouse I spilled oil and vinegar on; I took it to the dry cleaner, pointed out the spot, and mentioned what I had spilled on it. I was delighted to get it back with no evidence of my need for a bib. Hiding the spots so the dry cleaner doesn't know what a messy eater you are doesn't help him or her remove the spots.

Don't have your clothing dry cleaned more than necessary, certainly not after each use, unless you have a stain. Dry-cleaning chemicals are hard on the fabric and on you. Always remove the dry cleaning bag and dispose of it. Allow the clothing to air out before you wear it.

I have successfully hand washed or used the gentle cycle on my washing machine for silk blouses and sweaters. I even throw them in the dryer on no-heat to fluff out wrinkles and then hang or lay them flat to finish drying. Special delicate washing solutions are available from some finer department stores for washing silk. They are expensive, but considering the cost of replacing a silk blouse, they may be worth the investment. I have recently found some wonderful homemade laundry cleaners that are gentler and healthier for the environment. I am very happy with the results on my delicate fabrics.

Read your labels. I would never attempt to wash a blazer, unless the tag suggests it. Blazers that are not meant to be washed lose their defined shape very quickly in washing machines.

Warning: Frequent washing or dry cleaning of one piece in a suit combo will probably fade or slightly discolor that piece. BUT if you are wearing it frequently you are probably getting your money out of the piece. Just be aware of the possibly of fading and discoloration.

I once overheard a woman at *Ready for Success* comment that she did not want a linen suit because she couldn't afford to have it dry cleaned. Her shopper commented, "None of us can. Besides they wrinkle again so quickly. The thing with a linen suit Is that they give the appearance that you can afford to have them dry cleaned, so wearing them slightly wrinkled is acceptable."

Using a Steamer

Steamers are available on the retail market. If you have a large selection of suits between you and any male members of your household, the $80 investment quickly pays for itself in reducing dry cleaning costs. The steamer should be filled with cold distilled water. Plug it in, and wait for the steam to start to escape. It is important you hang the article of clothing as you work; the weight of the fabric will help to straighten out the wrinkles. Long strokes with the steamer are more effective than short ones. You may want to actually touch heavier fabrics with the steamer head. For lighter fabrics like silk, keep the steam head about two inches away. For embellished or very delicate items it is a good idea to steam the back of the fabric. For some heavier suit fabrics, steaming both the front and the back may be necessary. Drips and sputters from the steamer can be very frustrating; practice holding the hose straight down from the steamer head so the condensation runs back down the hose. When you are finished, hang the finished piece where air can circulate around it to remove the dampness. There are good and bad videos on the Internet on steaming. The tips I have offered here should help you discern the good from the bad.

Little Things that Count

- Smoking odors can be terribly offensive to nonsmokers. If you smoke, quit! Use the money you save to improve the quality of your wardrobe.
- Put used dryer sheets in a small plastic bag and carry them in your purse or car for a quick rub against your dress, skirt, pant leg, trouser socks, or panty hose to prevent static cling. Commercially available spray products are effective also.

- Pet hair can be difficult to remove, and it leaves the impression that you are careless about your presentation. With two dogs and two birds, I am always struggling with pet "give-aways" on my clothing. I carry a roller with tape wrapped around it to remove the hair before I leave my vehicle. These rollers are available from most discount stores. You can tear off sheets as they become covered with hair and lint, exposing a clean surface. Masking tape wrapped around your hand sticky-side-up also works very well. A retired military officer once approached me and said he had been taught not to do that with his wool dress uniform. The tape leaves a tacky build-up over time. He prefers a lint brush. He is probably right, but most women will not wear the same wool blazer for a decade.
- Don't stick nametags on leather or suede clothing. They will leave a mark and sticky residue when removed.
- Be sure to remove sticky nametags from your clothing before washing, as the washing removes the paper backing but leaves a sticky residue which is very difficult to remove.
- Need an emergency hem? Scotch tape works well for a temporary fix on most fabrics. If you are not handy with a needle and thread, fusible tape is available in sewing stores. Lay the tape along the edge of the fabric, fold over, and iron. The tape melts into place to hold the hem, even through several washings.
- Try a lint brush on heavier fabric with dried-on mud or food. It can sometimes be brushed off. This is the best choice for suede shoes, jackets, or handbags.
- The size of shoulder pads can really date a blazer or jacket, but removing shoulder pads from jackets and blazers is a risk. Usually the construction and cut of the jacket are dependent on the body the shoulder pads give the garment. Occasionally you can replace the big shoulder pads in jackets with smaller ones. Make certain doing so doesn't leave extra fabric wrinkling at the top of the garment.
- A good tailor is a valuable asset, especially if he or she is a friend or family member who may be willing to take things (like baked

goods) or services (like babysitting or pet walking) in trade for hemming, letting out seams, or narrowing pant legs. A good seamstress can reshape a piece of clothing that is slightly out-of-date into something more modern by, for example, cropping a longer jacket or narrowing the waist of a boxy blazer.

Button, Button, Who's Got the Button?

Missing buttons are details that can spoil a carefully crafted professional look in the blink of an eye. Pay attention to your buttons. Are they sewn on well? Reinforce them BEFORE the threads break and you lose the button. A little clear nail polish on the threads will strengthen where the threads rub against the holes of the button. If the color is not a problem, dental floss is a great reinforcement for buttons on heavy fabrics like coats.

- When wearing a double-breasted jacket, button the inside button first and the jacket will hang straighter. Think of David Letterman and his habit of unbuttoning and buttoning his inside button on his double-breasted jacket during his monologue.
- Lose a button to a special piece? If possible, move the bottom button to the top. It will be less noticeable if you use a slightly different button on the bottom. Or make the top button something totally different and eye-catching. It will appear to be intentional.
- Replacing poor quality or dressy buttons with more subdued ones will change the look of a blazer or jacket from dressy to more career casual.
- Many articles of new clothing come with extra buttons attached. If they are sewn inside the piece of clothing, leave them until you need them. If they come in a little packet attached to the tag, tear

them off and collect all of them in a glass jar with a lid. You might have to search through several to find the right one, but at least they are all in one place.

I once purchased a beautiful size 6 dress for $1.00 at a garage sale. It was obviously not my size, but the buttons were a perfect fit for the blazer I also bought that had ugly buttons. Buttons can be expensive to purchase new. Think about checking the secondary clothing market for just buttons.

Saving buttons from damaged clothing is a thrifty idea our grandmothers used. Remember all those button jars? Not a bad idea, even today!

CHAPTER EIGHT

And for the Ruben*esque* Woman

Peter Paul Rubens was a Flemish Baroque painter in the 17th century whose softly rounded women delighted the art world. This period in history glorified the well-endowed woman, with her curves and soft mounds of flesh. After all, it signified that she could afford to eat! So whether we are discussing Ruben*esque*, curvaceous, plus size, or big beautiful women, let's celebrate the gifts all of us have. Be a confident, capable, and successful woman, and dress that way! Thank you, Oprah!

Success Secret #17

I have yet to meet a woman who thinks she has the perfect body, whether she is size 6, 12, 16, or 24. We waste too much time and energy obsessing about our bodies! Remember the ads with supermodels are even retouched. Let's move on, ladies!

First let's clear up some terms and misconceptions in this area: size 16W does not mean 16 WIDE. It means 16 WOMEN. In the clothing industry, *W* means wide in reference to shoes only. Plus sizes refer to women's sizes that allow more room for the curves a woman may have, especially in the hips and bust. They are usually designed for wearers of size 14 and above. Not all size 16 or 18 clothing is created equally. A size 16 juniors is not the same as a 16 misses, nor is a 16 women's even close to the same fit. The sizes can even vary dramatically depending on the clothing manufacturer. Then we add petites and occasionally talls. Most stores separate the misses from juniors, sometimes even placing the women's department on another floor.

What if your tops are in one department and your bottoms in another? Many manufacturers have recognized the inconsistencies in sizing and have added such labels as "classic fit," "urban fit," or "modern fit" to further confuse the shopper. I like the idea of multiple cuts, but I can never remember if I am "modern fit" at Christopher & Banks or a "Marisa" at the Loft. Now do you understand why it takes a woman so long to shop? And why many women hate to shop?

Yet it is amazing how many women I work with have a difficult time trying on a garment labeled 18, especially if they are convinced they wear a 16. Women are sometimes shocked if I mention trying on a 16W. The addition of that one letter sends shivers of fear and shouts of "I'm not one of *those* women!" A 16W will generally be more generous in the hips and thighs for slacks (though the waist may need to be taken in) or the bust for tops, which may be just the room a woman needs. On the other side, a woman convinced she wears 16W pants may actually have a better fit in 18 misses if she is narrower in the hips. If the waist is too tight, it may be easier to have the hips taken in on the 16W. It is past the time for industry-wide standards of sizing in women's clothing. I have a few ideas, if they would only ask me!

While I am on the subject, petite sizes are generally not only shorter but also smaller in the waist, across the shoulders, in the rise, and around the hips. The difference can be three inches. So move up one to two sizes if you are a shorter woman but not petite all over.

Women of all sizes will frequently have trouble with suits paired in one size. Many women will vary a size or even several sizes between their tops and bottoms. There is nothing wrong with these women; it is the manufacturers and clothing stores who insist on selling matching tops and bottoms in sets rather than separates.

Ruben*esque* women have a reputation for being sloppy. Many of us wear our clothing too loose. Are we trying to hide something? Well, it ain't happening. We only look sloppy. And about that untucked blouse trying to hide our stomachs? We aren't fooling anyone! Tuck it in, blouse it slightly over the waistband, and look in the mirror. Doesn't that look more professional? I am glad that more tops are made today to be untucked. Depending on the blouse or top, try it out tucked and untucked while looking in the mirror. Which looks more finished?

And then at the other end of the fashion spectrum is the woman, usually a young woman more confident in her body, who is trying to wear the latest thing from the juniors department only in a size too small so that excess flesh rolls over the waistband and out from under the top. A V-neck top on a small-busted woman looks much different on a well-endowed woman. Take an honest look at yourself. Is your cleavage the first thing someone notices? This does not create an appropriate appearance for the work environment. Remember, there IS a difference between datewear and daywear! Of course, even a size 6 should not be showing the flesh between her top and bottom at work.

Ruben*esque* women can look as confident and professional as their slimmer counterparts, though I will admit it can be more of challenge and takes more work. The clothing industry is catching on that these beautiful women are seeking decent clothing. Unfortunately, just as very petite women (those who wear size 2) have trouble finding suitable clothing in mature styles, very large women are sometimes forced to choose fabrics and styles that are less than complimentary and professional in appearance.

Many upscale clothing manufacturers are designing and manufacturing improved options for the big, beautiful working woman. Those items are still very difficult to find in thrift stores, garage sales, and consignment stores. There has been somewhat of shift, and as women lose weight more plus size clothing is coming into the secondary market. However, in 1996, when I began my search for a navy blazer, I searched the secondary clothing market extensively for size 22. I found a few, but many were worn out or damaged beyond my ability to repair. It took me nearly six months of searching to find what I was looking for and, believe me, in those days I did not have the clothing experience I have now, nor my current standards of a good fit and quality clothing. Finding quality blazers in the moderately priced retail market is still a big challenge.

Dressing Tips

- Choose a solid color for your top and bottom; then layer a blazer or beautiful tailored open blouse over the top.
- Don't be afraid to try a short bolero jacket with pants or a skirt. I have had women swear they would expose too much of their "caboose" with such an outfit, yet when the blazer and bottom match in a solid color, the result can be very attractive.
- Stand up straight! Slouching only rolls the tummy out more and emphasizes the negative area.
- If you are one of the lucky ones with great legs, don't be afraid to show them with knee-length skirts—just not too short or too tight. You want to be able to sit down in them discreetly. Just below the knee is a great length.
- Draw attention to your face with a scarf, lovely pin, or necklace.
- If you are a plus petite, learn how to hem, or exchange services with someone who does. Maybe you could paint his or her kitchen! Keep your shoes, socks, and pants one color to add the illusion of height. If your waistband will be hidden, roll it to bring the crotch of the pants or hem of the skirt up to where it belongs.
- Find a good seamstress to work with. That way you can also shop with alteration possibilities in mind.
- Write down the names and labels that work for you. You may wish to search for this brand and size again, even online.

The retail choices are improving for Ruben*esque* women. There is power in our numbers and our dollars. As more women seek out suitable clothing options, demand better choices, and refuse to buy the unflattering merchandise offered in some women's departments, the buyers and designers will realize we like the same classic look as size 8 with just more a bit more material.

CHAPTER NINE

Organizing Your Closet to Save You Time and Money

I must admit that for many years I couldn't see the importance of organizing my closet. After all, I only owned a couple dresses and skirts. At *Ready for Success* we've had some wonderful volunteers who have not only taught me a lot about dressing but also about the importance of organization. You may not have hundreds of thousands of pieces of clothing pass through your closet in a year as we did, but knowing 1) what you have, 2) what needs to be replaced, and 3) where it is are real time and money savers.

Step One: Completely empty your closet!

- Does it need additional light? A higher wattage bulb can help. Battery operated lights are available; just be sure to turn them off. Can your closet be wired so the light comes on when you open the door?
- What color is the interior of your closet? A fresh coat of light-colored paint can really brighten a dim interior.
- Are the closet poles within your reach?
- Do you have shelves? Are they within your reach?
- Do you need space for shoes?
- Would a step stool help you reach the top shelves?

Many home-remodeling businesses and discount stores have closet organization systems for sale, and some offer personal advice on the best way to enhance the space and its use. It is possible to go online and plan various scenarios for an organized closet. Check out professional organizers in your area for ideas. What works best for your closet? It may be as simple as hanging two rods or moving a dresser into the closet. Don't forget to consider over-the-door systems.

Do you need more closet space? With the surge in flat screen TVs, used armoires are available on the secondary market. Do you have room to repurpose one into a closet space? A little paint, the addition of a closet pole, a few baskets, and perhaps drawer dividers will turn a used piece of furniture into a useful storage center.

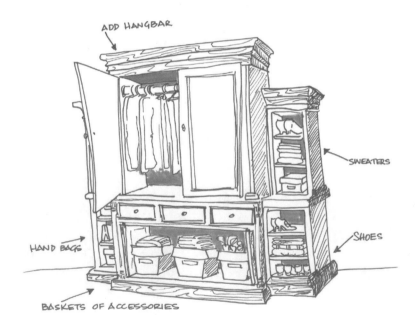

Step Two: Return the clothes to the closet!

- Check each piece over for necessary repairs. Mark the repairs with a safety pin or note and separate the piece into a repair pile.
- Check items for spots. Identify the spot. (I use a brightly colored painter's tape to prevent damage to the item.) If the item is washable, try a spot remover or pour white vinegar over it. Rewash and recheck before drying. Drying only sets most spots.

- Are the sweaters or t-shirts pilling or looking worn? These are items you can plan to replace at clearance sales.

Step Three: Be brutal!
- How long since you've worn this piece? You might have found a great deal on the sale rack but never really liked the color. Pass it along to someone who will. Maybe it is your size but is an uncomfortable fit, or the fabric is scratchy. Whatever it is that prevents you from wearing it, get rid of it. Make more room in your closet!
- Does it still fit? Many women I know have their "fat" clothes and their "thin" clothes. If it has been over a year since you have worn one or the other, get rid of them! You probably won't want those particular clothes if you gain or lose more weight anyway!
- If it is out of date, is there anything that could be done to update it? If not, get rid of it. I know women who hang on to clothing because they think the style will return. That is true, but the style will probably return with some new twist like different fabrics, colors, less or more shoulder pads, etc. Pass it along now while there is still some chance for someone else to get some wear out of it.

We attach great sentimental emotion to our clothing: the great deal we found, the outfit we bought with our sister on vacation, the outfit we were wearing when we got the promotion. The list goes on. Women bring in clothing all the time at *Ready for Success* that obviously had strong emotional meaning to the donor. That is one of the reasons clothing is sorted out of the eyesight of the donor. We fail to see the faults in our own clothing, especially those favorite pieces. So for this step, you must be brutal. Once you have sorted your clothing move on to Step Four.

Step Four: Sort by category.

Return your clothing to your clean, bright closet by hanging it together in sections: all your pants, all your skirts, all your blouses, and all your blazers. Then within each clothing type, divide your clothing into colors. I always separate the blacks and navy blues with a lighter color like khaki. I have learned by humbling experience that in the morning, black and navy can look the same. I have discovered after leaving the house that I am wearing a navy blue blouse with black pants, and that was not my intention!

Success Secret #18
Hang the pieces to your suits separately.
You will see them as separates with more choices of clothing partners within your closet.

I organize my shoes by season and then by color, after I check them for those needing repairs, polishing, and replacement. I use the top shelf in my closet for those things I only occasionally need, like a cardigan for a cool summer night. Those are things I don't want to have to move to my off-season storage place since I wear them much less frequently during that season. I usually keep my recreational wear (shorts, jeans, capris, and logo t-shirts) separate from my work wear. These can be folded and placed in dresser drawers.

Hangers

Did you realize hangers are not all created equal? Long-term clothing storage on wire hangers can create a strong, narrow crease in most clothing. And if exposed to moisture, wire hangers can leave unsightly rust marks on your clothing. Wire hangers frequently arrive in your home from the dry cleaner. If you prefer not to use them in your closet, ask if the dry cleaner will take them back to recycle or reuse. Leaving sweaters lying over the cardboard tube on a wire hanger can leave a light-colored mark on dark clothing. This mark can sometimes be vigorously brushed off. The best choice is to move the sweater to a plastic hanger, or better yet fold it and put it on a shelf or drawer.

I prefer wooden hangers. Plastic hangers are the next best choice. These are similar to the thin plastic ones used in most retail clothing stores. Finally plastic tube hangers are available inexpensively at most discount and dollar stores. These can come in many colors. When you purchase clothing ask if you can have the hanger. Many stores will add it to your bag or keep the clothing on it while putting the clothing in a garment bag. This also helps the clothing stay wrinkle free on the trip home from the store.

Hanging Tips

Many items with large neck openings will slip off hangers.

- Use wire hangers with foam covering.
- Use plastic retail hangers with no-slip pads at the ends.
- Slip the top into the hanger slots provided on some plastic and tube hangers.
- Use wooden clip clothes pins to hold the clothing in place.
- Use safety pins or straight pins to hold the clothing on the hanger.
- Use the long hanger ribbons that come attached to clothing with this problem. I typically dislike these ribbons and often cut them off. They tend to peek out of clothing at inappropriate times.

If you have those annoying "hanger bumps" (marks left in knit items), lay a damp cloth over the fabric while you are wearing the item of clothing. The dampness should relax the material.

When hanging pants and skirts, a crease can form if you fold them over a wire hanger, let alone the rusty wire mark already mentioned. Try folding them over a plastic tube hanger. The broader support leaves fewer marks. I prefer using clips to hang my pants and skirts. They allow me to hang these items without folding. Plastic clips to go on tube hangers to convert them to pant or skirt hangers can be purchased from discount stores. Again, wooden clothes pins or safety pins work also. Wooden and plastic hangers made specifically for pants and skirts can also be found in discount stores. They have a clasp set up to hold the pants between two bars. I hang all my pants folded at the waist to match the front crease of the pants. I like to hang my pants from the waist. Others prefer matching the seams and hanging the pants upside down from the hem. If I am short on hangers for pants and skirts, my better wear goes on the nicer hangers. I fold jeans and my casual wear on a shelf or in a drawer. If your waistline is considerably bigger than the hanger, fold the edges around to meet the clips. Hanging a skirt with a lot of extra fabric hanging off the sides allows many fabrics to stretch and affect your hemline.

I use short plastic covers over clothing that tends to collect dust on the shoulders. A lint brush can quickly remove the dust on most clothing, except beaded tops, some wool, and silk.

If you happen to have a window in your closet, beware of leaving silk exposed to sunlight. Sunlight fads and discolors the fabric quickly.

Step Five: Think seasonally savvy!

Do you live in an area of the country where there are drastic differences between seasons? Do you have room in your closet for summer and winter season wardrobes? I don't, so I acquired a sturdy portable rack I place in a dry storage area for my off-season clothing. I moved an old dresser nearby and place winter sweaters with sachet bags scattered about the drawers. Plastic storage bins work very well in place of a dresser. I place pieces of cedar from a friend's remodeled cedar closet near the rack, hoping to prevent moth and insect infestation. I use a flat storage box on small wheels under the bed for off-season shoes.

Decide which things in your wardrobe are definitely winter or summer. Transitional pieces are sometimes a little harder to make decisions about. Move the off-season things to your designated storage space. Twice a year you will switch the clothing. This is a perfect opportunity to re-examine the clothing you are keeping.

For these long-term storage things:

- Hang items on plastic hangers. Wire ones will sometimes leave rust marks over the long term.
- Remove all dry cleaner bags. Trapping those chemicals in your clothes is not a good idea.
- Cover the clothing with a clean sheet or old tablecloth to protect it from dust.
- Be sure the area is dry and free of mold.

Organization Is Its Own Reward

By having an organized closet I have a clearer picture of what I have to wear. By looking in the closet I can see where the gaps might be. Everything in my closet must have at least three buddies to justify its closet space. I actually save money with an organized closet. I can see that I now need to replace a white silk tank top I spilled a little spaghetti sauce on (and even with spot remover is not coming out), so I am keeping my eyes open at sales for such a top. I encourage sale shopping but not for the sake of collecting more clothing. Sale shopping will assist you in building a work wardrobe at reduced costs while upgrading the quality.

CHAPTER TEN

I Get the Idea, but I Still Can't Afford It!

In my search for a new way to present myself, I faced the hardest question of all. How can I afford better clothing when I can't afford food or clothing for my children? I certainly could not justify paying full price, even at discount stores. I began searching out great clothing deals and allowing a small amount as my clothing budget. I discovered that the better I was at bargain shopping, the better I was able to dress my children using those same skills. Of course, the more employable I saw myself, the more financial rewards there would be, the more my children would benefit. So where did I begin?

Fine Department Stores

Are you surprised to see that first on my list? I was too, as a novice clothing shopper! I will admit that shopping at the fine department stores takes a little bit more time, but the rewards can be awesome! I once felt too intimidated to even walk around a store I knew I could not afford to shop in. But, as I grew accustomed to visiting them on my research trips, I discovered their hidden secrets. I frequently find high-quality panty hose for a dollar on the clearance racks of these department stores. Don't be afraid to ask the clerk if they have any clearance or where their clearance items are. I find great bargains at the end-of-season sales on name brands in all sizes, even in my large size.

Scout out department stores that attract you. Spend an afternoon just wandering about the store and familiarizing yourself with the layout. These stores will usually have high-end merchandise as well as moderately priced merchandise departments. Familiarize yourself with the brand names in each area.

Smile and look directly at the sales associates when they speak to you. Developing a relationship with sales associates can make your shopping experience much easier, more pleasant, and more rewarding. I have also discovered that many of these high-end stores retain their associates longer, so you can work with the same person on future visits. Remember, they are working just as hard as you are to earn a living. If you have a particularly good person helping you, ask for her card. You can call and talk to her directly with questions about merchandise. Associates appreciate calls or online comments to the store complimenting them for a job well done. Sales associates will usually share with you…

- what they may know about upcoming sales.
- when they put their sale items out.
- how to put your name on the store mailing list.

You will probably not spend your money at these stores, except possibly on clearance items, so try not to be too demanding. Hang your clothes back on the proper hangers and place them on the racks provided in the dressing area. The staff frequently prefers to return tried-on items to the sale floor to avoid confusion. If the associates are busy, relax and enjoy the visit. Look around until they can get to you. Believe me, they will appreciate your patience.

Your Shoes Will Give You Away
I have had women tell me they felt associates in some of the high-end stores did not always treat them respectfully. I don't go to my favorite department store if I just finished gardening. In other words, be clean and presentable. Jeans are perfectly acceptable today, but put on clean and decent shoes. One associate I work with frequently told me she can tell by a customer's shoes how serious

he or she is about shopping in that department. I have to be honest, I did not realize in the beginning of my own search for a professional appearance just how much my shoes were saying about me.

Research – Another Name for Window Shopping

Remember, department stores are your research. Adding a statement in the current fashion color can be fun and will update your basic wardrobe. I found a bright lime-green blouse on sale for very little money that I wore under my navy blazer. Adding the new color to an old dependable piece updated the whole look. Keep in mind the name brands, fabrics, and types of construction you find in the finer department stores. The more educated and informed you are, the more confidence you will have to search for the next level of quality business clothing: the consignment shop.

Success Secret #19

Don't buy it, no matter how great the deal is, if…

- it is the wrong size today even if you are on a diet.
- the color isn't good on you.
- it's the right size but a poor fit for your body type.
- it needs alterations, unless the store offers them for free or you do that type of thing regularly. Don't just add it to your pile to do someday.
- it is still more than your budget allows, unless you will wear it enough times to justify the cost.

The Consignment Shop

Consignment shops usually take gently used clothing from customers and resell it, returning a percentage of the sale to the person who brought in the merchandise. Many of these stores are located in upscale areas, but not all. Consignment shops are usually very selective about what they take in.

- Clothes must be in the best possible shape—nearly new. You can research the approximate age of a piece of clothing by the manufacturer's tag inside.

- They could actually be new, something never even worn.
- They must be recent or current styles and trends. (An exception here is in retro and antique clothing.)

If you're bringing items in, call ahead to find out what season they are taking clothing for and how it should be brought in (always clean and usually on hangers). These stores usually send out checks on a monthly or quarterly basis for merchandise that was purchased, or they allow credit to be applied toward shopping in the store. In fact, a better percentage of the sale will be applied to store credit. Some consignment stores take other merchandise besides clothing including jewelry, handbags, even household appliances or knick-knacks. To be honest, I still have found better deals on clearance racks at fine department stores than at consignment stores. Nevertheless, these businesses offer better quality and prices than the usual discount store. Ask to be on their mailing list, if they have one. Remember these stores have new things coming in on a daily basis. Many consignment stores lower the prices on items that have been there longer than 60–90 days.

Find a consignment shop with prices and quality you like and in an area that is easy for you to get to. Most of these businesses are clean and set up with dressing rooms and a return policy. Then stop by on a regular or semi-regular basis. Don't expect to find something every time you go; however, on occasion, someone with your similar taste and size will have brought in clothing that could fill your shopping bag and budget easily.

The associates in many of these stores are owners, part owners, or long-time employees. Take the time to get to know them. Let them know the kinds of things you are seeking. I have found some lovely formal wear that had obviously been only worn once for special occasions in these stores.

Moderately Priced Stores and Specialty Shops

These stores will frequently advertise wonderful clearance offers. Most of them are great deals on good products, but pay attention to the details of the offer.

Success Secret #20
Sometimes a sale or bargain is not one!
Do the math of a sale.

I have frequently found sale signs advertising clothing for 30%–50% off, yet when I examine the price and really look at the clothing, I recognize it as not that great of a deal. In calculating the sale price, consider these factors:

- Does the percentage off apply to the original price of the article or current markdown price?
- Is the sale price already marked or will it be taken at the register?
- To "quick estimate" the price at the clearance rack, figure what 10% would be. If the price is $19.99 and the article is 30% off, round $19.99 up to $20. 10% of $20 is $2, times 3; thus it would be about $6 off or a total price of just over $14.
- 80% off? I reverse the earlier suggestion: 10% of $20 is $2, times 2 equals $4 as the total price.
- 50% off? Divide the price in half. 75% off? Divide 50% off in half again.
- Don't forget the tax.
- Watch the register as your purchase is rung up. Was the price what you expected? If not, why not? It is easier to handle differences at the register rather than coming back later.

I have spent thousands of dollars for the *Ready for Success* program on discounted items, and the errors have been numerous! It is worth my time and yours to be sure computer scanners are working properly, clothing is on the right rack, and sale signs are accurate. Politely question the differences.

Men's Stores or Departments

Consider shopping men's stores or departments. Usually the tailoring is free. Buttons are traditionally on the other side from women's clothing, but honestly, who will notice? And men's shirts are cheaper to dry clean. Men's sizes are more exact, and for the plus size women, it's easier to find larger sizes. Pants in the men's department are not always a good choice for women if the crotch area is cut differently.

Discount Stores

The industry has begun to realize that carrying clothes for business casual makes good financial sense. These stores have always carried very good collections of recreational and informal wear at low prices and are good places to pick up a plain, no-pocket t-shirt in a new fashion color or a basic white or black top to wear under a cardigan, blazer, or vest. The basic khaki pant can be found here reasonably, especially if you don't have the time to search for your size and price range on the sale rack of the department store.

Outlet Stores

Name brand stores and merchandise open these stores to entice their usual buyers and introduce discount shoppers to their products. They may carry catalog returns as well as last season's items that didn't do as well as the store buyers expected. Great deals can be found here, but I have still found better deals in the clearance departments of finer department stores; I just have to work harder to find them. One lingerie manufacturer has an outlet near me offering bras at discounted prices, yet I found the same bras on a clearance rack of my favorite department store at half the price being offered by the outlet store. Of course, the price at the outlet mall was 30% off the full price. With practice you will learn which of your favorite products may be found with some regularity for a reasonable price at outlets. I am not a big enough fan of outlet malls to drive a great distance and shop all day. However, if I still lived in a more rural area I would appreciate them more. I will stop if I am driving by one.

Estate Sales

Estate sales or moving sales are usually better for other types of shopping rather than clothing. The professionals who handle up-scale sales tell me antique clothing and some upscale clothing will sell. They themselves are frequently searching for someplace to send their leftovers or even the pre-sale clothing. These sales usually involve one woman or a family; therefore, you would be lucky to find your size and style preference. BUT, it does happen. If the family themselves are handling the estate sale, they may be willing to negotiate on prices, but this is rarely the case if they are using a dealer. You might try leaving your name and number if things don't sell and you think the clothing would be a real asset to your closet. Be forewarned. My experience is the family or dealer wants you to take it all at the end of sale, not just pick through for a few pieces. Still these are great places to find silk scarves, costume jewelry, nice handbags, and briefcases.

Thrift Stores

These stores normally sell items to support some type of non-profit organization, church, or mission. People donate items and in return they receive a tax write-off. Not everyone is interested in the tax write-off; many people are only seeking a worthwhile agency to support with their clothing or other donations. Frequently the employees here are volunteers or the limited paid staff is supplemented by volunteer help. They may also be working in some type of retail training program.

The prices might compare with garage sale prices except...

- usually the weather is less of a factor when shopping.
- the stores have regular hours of operation.
- the stores have dressing rooms, or they should.
- the products come from more varied resources; thus, there are more choices.

Thrift shops can vary widely in quality, quantity, and cleanliness of items. The merchandise changes on an almost daily basis.

I encourage you to seek out one near you that meets your standards of organization and cleanliness, and then stop by frequently. I found one thrift store that did not offer a dressing room and did not take returns. I never went back. Normally these types of businesses do not negotiate on price. They will have great clearance prices or specials, depending on the size of their inventory. Ask if they have a frequent shopper program or online discount coupons.

These stores are often seeking help. Depending on the store policy for volunteer purchases, this can be a great opportunity with the additional perk of allowing you regular shopping of their merchandise. (Don't forget to list volunteering on your resume.)

Garage Sales, Yard Sales, and Church Rummage Sales
I have a long history of garage *sailing*. My car has logged thousands of miles searching garage sales. *Sailing* can be visiting your favorite areas at the end of the week and watching for the ever-present yard sign. It can also be an organized sport. Check local papers, and don't forget online sources. Gather your map and mark your route. Arrive early for the best selection but less opportunity to haggle. This sport can be fun with friends, especially if you are seeking different things. An extra set of eyes in a dim garage is very helpful. Be prepared and carry cash. You could organize a garage sale weekend on your street or in your town. Just be sure to have extra help to staff your garage sale so you have time to shop the others.

My daughters and I have found some amazing things at garage sales, from children's clothing to beautiful furniture. Adult clothing is a more difficult area in which to score big at garage sales. Once again you are dealing with only one woman or a small group of women, so ask when you walk up the drive if they have the size you are searching for.

Garage Sale Shopping Tips

- Measure the shoulder width, sleeve length, pant length, inseam length, rise length, and waist of a favorite blouse or top and pair of slacks. Write down the numbers and carry them in your purse.
- Carry a tape measure to check clothing without trying it on. You can compare the numbers with your list from your favorite pieces, although trying it on is still the best choice. This trick works well for other members of your family too, who may not be into garage *sailing*.
- Ask if you can carry the article of clothing out into the sunlight to check for stains. Many of these types of sales are held in dark garages or poorly lit areas.
- Remember it is very rare to be able to return something for a refund to a garage sale. So if it doesn't work, how much will you be losing when you donate it to a thrift store, sell it at your own garage sale, or sell it online?

Church rummage sales are usually a great source of adult clothing and accessories because multiple families are involved. They sometimes also have sections for different types of clothing. Several annual sales I am very familiar with have special areas for upscale items and designer names. Discounts are usually offered on the last day.

It Never Hurts to Ask

My standard rule of thumb at a garage sale is to always ask if they will take less for the item. Then suggest a price. Even if they say no, you can walk away knowing you got the best possible deal they would offer on the article. Leave your name and number in case they reconsider your offered price and the item is important enough to you. Or go on down the road and possibly find it cheaper. The last day of the sale, as with an estate sale, is the very best time to negotiate. If you are purchasing several things from the same sale, ask for a discounted price on all of the things as a group.

Clothing Swaps

Clothing swaps are becoming more popular. Usually a group of people get together and ask everyone to bring new or nearly new clothing. This is a great chance for you to rid your closet of those irresistible sale items that never worked. This system works best with a large networking circle. Then depending on the number of items you brought in, you can shop the racks to take home the same number. These can be very fun when organized around a tea or a lunch and sometimes a speaker. A small fee could be charged to cover the cost of the speaker, room, and food. Left-over clothing is usually donated to a charity. Take your tape measure when attending one of these events.

eCommerce

When I first wrote *Dress to Impress*, online business was just budding. Now it is a full-fledged bloom affecting all of us, even if we don't have a computer. Businesses offer coupons, specials, and discounts only on the Internet, which, unfortunately, leaves the computer-less out in the cold. Fewer newspapers print fewer ads, and the computer savvy shopper probably had the ad a day or two earlier than the print release. There are worlds of shopping only available on the Internet, quite literally at our fingertips: Craigslist, eBay, Etsy, etc. The online business world is also affecting the actual physical world of shopping. Most businesses offer some sort of online business, decreasing actual square footage in stores.

While many of us continue to like to actually touch and feel products before we buy, a world of free shipping and easy returns is changing even seasoned shoppers. You can shop any time of the day or night, with no waiting in lines or fighting crowds. No one will see your shoes or your pajamas. The department store research I have suggested can be very valuable here. If you know the size and brand that fits you perfectly, searching the Internet for the item in your budget just became much easier. If you are in a hurry, try ordering the product from a nearby store and picking it up the same day.

Paying for your order now demands access to a credit card, a debit card, or at the very least a bank account. This side of eCommerce can be daunting to people just starting out with less access to plastic. Paypal offers to withdraw payments for purchases directly from your bank account, if you have one. It is also possible to now preload credit cards (some businesses accept only one or two types) and gift cards (though this limits where you can shop) with cash. Read the fine print to check for fees and time limits when using these methods.

If you don't have access to your own computer and web connection, try your local library. Check their policies for usage and online shopping. Many public schools and community education programs offer classes in computer usage to the general public. Workforce programs in your area should have resource centers with computer access available.

If there are any Internet beginners left, here are some tips to get started:

- Use a search engine (Google, Yahoo!) to find a particular clothing company or brand.
- Choose a site and browse their offering. eBay has very clear tips and instructions on their site for using their services. Find out what the abbreviations mean to save you time and effort.
- The more specific you are in your search, the less overwhelming the choices become. Try several different descriptions of clothing articles, including size and color.
- Are there shipping charges or sales tax? With these additional charges, it may not be the great deal it appears to be at first.

How to Pay for It?

Like anything, it is easy to get caught up in the excitement of finding a great clothing deal. I admit that when I began my search for an improved wardrobe, I could not afford groceries. I had two teenage daughters also in need of clothing and wanting the latest fashion trend like their friends. Figuring out how to afford clothing for myself was a real challenge. I was struggling to maintain and find a financial balance with a budget with very little room for error or mistakes! I had declared bankruptcy with the divorce, had no credit cards, and a very poor credit history. I began a serious effort to slowly work my way out of that hole I was in. I limited my clothing purchases to a few dollars a month. I let friends and family know I was seeking clothing in my size. I had to be honest what my size was. Shortly after we began *Ready for Success*, two very dear friends blessed me with a shopping trip. They took me to stores, bought me clothing, bras, panties, camisoles, shoes, and even a coat! It was an amazing experience for me personally. I am not sure if my two friends ever realized how important that shopping trip was for me.

Slowly over time, paying bills on time, trying not to overextend myself, asking for help with a grateful heart for specific things from family and friends, I reached a point where I could see daylight! I now have credit cards, a decent credit rating, and a retirement plan!

Credit Tips

- Talk to your creditors. Be upfront about problems you may be facing.
- Offer your creditors a pay-off plan, and then stick to it or call them before they call you if the plan fails.
- Shop with a list and stick to it!
- Set a dollar amount for all purchases, including gifts, groceries, gas, and clothing. Don't forget to include all these categories in your budget. These variables are places we sometimes try to really cut corners and then fail.
- Be upfront with your children and other family members. In order for a budget to work, everyone needs to be on the same page and understand the situation.
- Don't be afraid to seek help from other sources. Those resources are there to help and will appreciate you working hard to overcome your problems. According to my sources in social services,

the majority of people using these services usually use them only an average of two years to overcome difficult situations. In very difficult economic times that has extended, just as the number of people needing services has increased.
- Coupons are wonderful for a product you need, will use, and can afford, but only under those conditions.
- Consider volunteering to help you build references, recommendations, work experiences, or any skills you want to develop. Helping someone else is a great way to get your mind off your own troubles. You might enjoy it or even find a new career! You will make great contacts and good friends!
- Consider bartering. Do you know someone who sews and who might appreciate a babysitter, housecleaner, or closet organizer?

Being creative and resourceful can help you weather life's storms. Hopefully reading this book will open you to a good idea or two.

CHAPTER ELEVEN

The Blending of Many Cultures and Gifts

We have worked with women from many different cultures at *Ready for Success*. Our volunteers are also from a variety of cultures and ethnic backgrounds. In America, the globalization of business and the expansion of a multicultural, multiracial workforce have broadened the acceptance of ethnically diversity in clothing in many companies. Not only in this country but also worldwide, the diversity of dress around the world is actually melting into few limitations of business dress. Traditional business attire is sometimes more "westernized" than other forms of dress within the same country. The business casual dress world has opened up, recognized, and allowed for more personal choice. Today many women wish to keep the clothing and customs of their native lands. Yet I have also met numerous women from other countries who tell me they want to dress more "Western."

There have always been religious sects within our culture that require the women to dress more modestly than most Americans. These differences have become less obvious with the freedom of choice the business casual world has brought. Even as the pendulum swings to a more professional look, the choice of skirts rather than pants and longer skirts rather than short skirts makes personalized dress less noticeable.

Some cultures expect a woman to be fully covered, exposing

only her eyes. Some Americans see this as extreme. For many women and men it represents the repression of women, and this angers their sense of what is acceptable. The individual woman herself in that very traditional dress may not feel that way at all. Her traditional dress is a statement of her faith. She finds comfort in taking the focus from her sexuality and body to her intellectual gifts. Recently college campuses have seen young women expressing this very view.

At the less extreme end of the spectrum we find long skirts, long sleeves, and headscarves (hijab) that meet religious and political expectations and are easier to accept by our culture in general. I spoke with a young Muslim woman at a recent workshop. She was wearing a long skirt, ankle boots, long sleeves on her jacket, and her head was wrapped with a beautiful scarf. She said she had been born in America and liked dressing to honor her faith, but she was much more casual about it than her father was. She giggled and showed how the slit of her skirt exposed the calf of her leg. Sounds like the relationship of any young daughter and her father concerning her clothes.

A woman wrapped in yards of beautiful blue silk came into *Ready for Success.* "I want to try on pants; I have never worn pants," she said. While the volunteers "oh'd" and ah'd" over her gorgeous costume, they did find her a wonderful classic pant and blazer combination. She was delighted. Whether or not she ever wore that suit out in public doesn't matter; she wanted to see herself in a new way.

When women from other cultures tell me they want to dress more "Western" yet stay within the confines of their sense of cultural appropriateness, here are some suggestions I offer:

• Americans have a strong sense of what colors go together and what is appropriate for combinations of prints, stripes, and plaids. Women from other cultures select combinations we see as odd. I will suggest to the woman if she wants to look more "Western" that perhaps we could mix another combination, but only if

she wants to. I personally like the vibrant choices some cultures choose.
- What are the limits of their dress code? Some women will accept skirts slightly above the ankle if they have ankle boots to hide the ankle. Some will accept short sleeves or no sleeves if there is some type of blouse or jacket worn over it.

As with all of us, what is beautiful is answered by our experiences, our culture, and our personal choices. In some African American groups a well-rounded derrière is considered beautiful, so a tight skirt or pant is more acceptable.

At *Ready for Success* we noticed that some refugees and immigrants have a very strong sense of fabric and clothing construction. They are sometimes appalled with our acceptance of poor construction and disregard for cheap fabrics in our business casual clothing. They have a higher standard of quality.

Dressing more "Western" has been a great equalizer for immigrants and refugees throughout our history. It certainly helps women assimilate quickly into our culture. We also have an equally long tradition of accepting other modes of dress (the Amish, some Jewish sects). Fortunately there is room for both in America. Modesty, cleanliness, and attractiveness are more important criteria in any form of dress.

One area I encourage woman to overcome is the cultural training of their body language that in this country is misunderstood:

- Not smiling or covering their mouth when they smile
- Downcast eyes
- Whispering their name
- Limply shaking hands

When I work with women in some cultural groups, giggling and laughter abound as we seek a way to respect each woman's lifetime of training and habit. Sometimes the women just need to know that in Western society it is acceptable for a woman to present herself more powerfully.

It is sometimes challenging to work with a woman who has a dress code so different than mine and complicated by language barriers, but warm smiles and hugs cross all boundaries of understanding.

CHAPTER TWELVE

And for the Men...

When Episcopal Community Services decided to add a *Men's Ready for Success* program, I was thrilled and happy to volunteer. I admit I had some misconceptions about working with men that were dispelled on my first day. I assumed that it would be easier, take less time, and be met with more guarded enthusiasm than working with women. My first client was just as selective about the quality of clothing as any woman; he strutted and preened in front of the mirror, just as any woman; he was just as discriminating about color combinations; his smile was just as big; and his hug was maybe even tighter than any woman I have ever worked with.

I decided to add this chapter because so many men depend on the women in their lives to worry about how they look. One young man I worked with asked if he could wear his new suit home. "Of course," was my reply. He said, "I want to stop by my grandmother's. She is going to be crying and carrying on about how nice I look." I am sure her reaction did not disappoint him. The truth is, it was how HE felt when he looked in the mirror—as HE imagined how others would view this new him—that really mattered. That was the reason I added this new chapter.

The same reasons why it is important for a woman to know how to present herself in a professional manner apply to any man. Read Chapter 1 as if I was speaking to a man. One of the real differences between men and women is that men are willing to copy their peers and superiors. A friend who worked in HR once told me about the small company she worked for with three male owners. Monday, one owner wore a sweater vest, and by the end of the next week, both other partners were wearing sweater vests. And by the end of the month, every man in the company wore a sweater vest. This is exactly why suits caught on 200 years ago and continue today in a slightly different version.

But before I talk about suits, let's start at the very beginning.

Personal Grooming

Bathing or showering regularly seems obvious to some, but the trick here is the regularity. Please shower or bathe more than once a week. Every other day is a much better choice. If you work hard, play hard, smoke, or just perspire a lot, a quick daily shower will do you more good than harm. If dry skin is a concern with all that water, then try lotion, especially on your hands, feet, and face. It does not have to be the scent the woman in your house prefers or the smell you prefer on her. Cornhuskers, Neutrogena, and Gold Bond Ultimate all make lotion with a more neutral scent. Try a pumice stone on those rough, dry heels, and there is nothing wrong with mixing up a batch of Nana's Sugar Scrub (see Chapter 7) for your hands and feet.

A good haircut will help any man look his best; in addition, remember while you are in the shower to wash your hair. Do your eyebrows, ears, and nose hairs need to be trimmed? I know I am getting a little personal, but those kinds of things can draw negative attention at the all-important first impression.

Facial Hair

The latest trends with actors and musicians is an unkempt beard of some sort. If you are a musician or actor and don't need a day job too, you can skip this part. But if not, I am certain you learned to use a razor. Lather, shave with the hair growth, rinse the blade, and shave carefully against the hair grain. Continue around your face and neck. If you think a mustache adds to your appearance, please keep it out of your mouth. A beard can be very nice on a man, if it is short, and here I mean trimmed to less than one-half an inch or shorter. To be brutally honest, if you are job hunting, clean-shaven is the best choice. When you get the job, find out about the dress code. Even then, look around. Do you see any other men with facial hair? I had a gentleman I was coaching at the workforce center challenge me about his facial hair. I didn't say he had to cut it off. I simply asked if it limited his job offers, was he willing to keep it?

Skip the heavily scented aftershave. Your goal is NOT to announce yourself before you enter the room and then allow your scent to linger when you leave. Besides, with today's awareness of scent allergies many places discourage colognes. If you are bathing regularly, there should be no need anyway.

Tattooed, Pierced, Gauged
Once you have tattoos or gauged earlobes, they are hard to remove without leaving the signs of their existence. Jeff Strickler, a writer for the *Star Tribune*, published a story entitled "The Case Against Stretching Earlobes." Strickler interviewed several young men for the article, and one stated it clearly: "It's not that I regret it [stretching the lobes], but this is a different time in my life….If I want to be taken seriously as a professional, I have to start looking like a professional. Whether you like it or not, or whether it's fair or not, people judge you based on your appearance" (2012, para. 1). This young man is about to undergo plastic surgery to return his earlobes to a more "normal" appearance. He has decided his 10-year project of ear lobe enlargement (gauging) is at an end.[2]

---

2   Jeff Strickler. "The Case Against Stretching Earlobes." Star Tribune, January 24, 2012, http://www.startribune.com/lifestyle/137908688.html.

I once attended a volleyball tournament with my daughters. The facility had a great gift shop marketing to volleyball players and their parents. A young man who worked there on weekends had multiple piercings on his face. The patterns were very artistic and amazing. However, the whole time I kept wondering, "I bet it really hurts to get hit in the face with a volleyball!" I was so distracted, I forgot what I came in to purchase, equaling a lost sale.

My brother who as a teenager had the most beautiful white-blonde hair growing well below his shoulders, refused to give permission for his teenage son to get a piercing. "You can cut your hair, but remember someday you may be sitting in a board meeting across from an old man like me, and I'll notice that earring." My brother still has great hair, but it's short now.

I have worked with both men and women who nervously try to cover the tattoos on their hands. Those tattoos represented a life they wanted desperately to leave behind. Make-up works sometimes, but the best removal is done by a plastic surgeon.

Hands and Nails
Remember the all-important handshake. If you need a refresher on shaking hands see Chapter 7.

Are your hands clean? If you were working on your motorcycle the night before, use the fingernail brush and GOOP. Clean them up, gentlemen! Trim your nails even with your fingertip, leaving just a crescent of white. You can file back and forth, but the little file in your nail clipper is not the best choice. The drug store will carry thick emery boards to make the job quicker. Using the right tool will save time. If you are uncertain about hand and nail care, visit a manicurist, and then keep the nail pattern the professional laid out.

Now that you're clean and ready, I'll leave the boxer or briefs choice up to you. T-shirts are a great idea, especially in cold weather. If they are to be seen, such as a round neck t-shirt under a V-neck sweater, be sure they are clean. A colored t-shirt peeking out from under that V-neck sweater is a better choice than the white one.

Clothing Choices

The Suit

The best advice I have is to purchase the finest navy suit you can afford. A suit consists of a jacket and pants in the same color and fabric. The best choice of fabric is probably mid-weight wool. A three-piece suit is even better, as it offers the additional vest to add to your wardrobe. Many businesses catering to men's suits will offer in-house tailoring. Suits are sized by the width of the chest and a man's height. It can be confusing. The Men's Wearhouse has information on sizing men's suits on their website. Just for your information, a "bespoke" is a custom-made suit, which usually requires several fittings and is more expensive.

The fit of your suit will say a lot about you.

- Your sleeves should hit your wrist bone when standing with your arms to your side.
- The shoulders of the suit should not be too heavily padded. A more relaxed natural slope to the shoulder is the standard now.

- The edge of the jacket shoulder should line up perfectly with where your arm drops down from your shoulder.
- If the blazer has a pleat or pleats, it should lie closed when you are standing.
- Can you button the button without pulling the fabric or popping the button while you are standing?

While we are on the subject of buttons:

- I would suggest a two-button suit as your first choice. Only button the top button, never the bottom.
- A three-button suit is buttoned in the middle.
- The double-breasted suit is always buttoned on the inside before buttoning the outside button.
- The single-button suit is cut higher to allow it to be buttoned.
- The general rule of thumb is to leave the bottom button unbuttoned.

It is a good idea to unbutton your suit when you sit down to prevent, as Gary Veazie, the Program Director of *Men's Ready for Success*, says, the danger of flying buttons!

Your suit should last for years and carry you to job interviews, weddings, and social occasions of all types. You can use all the pieces together or use them separately with other articles of clothing. This is your base.

Plan on dry cleaning it once or twice a year, hang it up to air out after every use, and learn to use a steamer. See Chapter 7 for tips on steaming and caring for your clothes. A former military officer once shared this tip with me at a workshop: A clothing brush is better for a man's suit than masking tape or sticky products to remove lint, pet hair, or dust. Eventually the stickiness will leave a residue on the suit.

Next, acquire a gray suit, or a nice sports coat. A sports coat is a jacket only and is more casual than a suit. In the beginning, select a sports coat that is simple; the fabric may have more texture than the suit, or even more pattern. I would not suggest too much pattern for your first sports coat. You will look great by just throwing the jacket on over anything from jeans and a t-shirt to khakis and a thin sweater. That step alone moves you to career casual.

Tips for shopping the secondary market for suits or blazers:

- Know your size; sometimes the size label is hidden in the inside pocket.
- If you have found the nearly perfect suit at a secondary market, a good tailor or seamstress should be able to fit the suit to you. Skip it if the armholes are too small. That is the hardest thing to change.
- Look it over for puckers on the lapel. Fusing gives the suit its structure. If that fusing gets wet in the rain it will pucker. Ironing or dry cleaning cannot correct it. Pass on it.
- Smell the blazer; mothballs, strong perspiration odors, and cigar smoke can be more trouble to remove than the jacket is worth.

Pants
Flat front pants are much more contemporary. However, many men, especially if they have a little extra weight around the middle, find pleated fronts more comfortable to sit in. The pleats should lay flat when you are standing. We have already established the navy suit and the matching pair of pants in your wardrobe. Where you are working and the job you have will determine the next pant purchase. Additional dress pants are important for any job working in the financial industry, upscale retail, and for interviews where a suit may not be necessary. Dockers or khakis are the pant of choice for business casual. Please note I do not mean dirty, wrinkled, faded, or cargo pants with multiple pockets. Save these for your weekend wear.

The pants should not be dragging on the ground. NO EXCUSES! Find a tailor, a friend who sews, or learn yourself from videos on the Internet. Maybe you could trade yard work services for a neat look to the bottom of your pants. Dress pants can be a touch longer in the back than the front, with a "break" at your shin when you are standing straight, meaning the pant has a slight indentation below the knee and above the ankle. Dockers and jeans can have a little extra length to them.

Pants should be hung up either folded at the waist with creases matching using clips or with side seams matching and hung from the cuff using a bar pant hanger. Pants can be folded and hung over a plastic tube hanger, but this tends to leave creases across the knees or thigh area.

Belts hold up your pants. USE THEM! Invest in a good leather belt one inch to one and half inches wide with a simple buckle. Belts should be used around your waist not your hips.

Tips on buying pants on the secondary market:
- Check the zippers to be sure they work. Zippers can be replaced but the pants must be worth the effort.
- Check that the fabric in the crotch is not excessively worn or pilling.

Shirts

"I am not wearing a dress shirt! The last one I had almost choked me to death!" Shirts are sized by neck size and length of arm. If you can't breathe, perhaps you need to try a larger neck size. You should be able to place two fingers side-by-side between the collar and your neck with the collar buttoned. It is also possible to get small elastic button extenders to give you a bit more room. Is it going to feel like a t-shirt? No. The collar button should be buttoned if you are wearing a tie, unless you just got off work. Otherwise, wearing an unbuttoned (the collar button) dress shirt without a tie and a nice pair of pants or Dockers does create the acceptable business casual look in many companies.

Use collar stays. They are they small plastic strips that help give structure to your collar. Most dress shirts will have a little slot for them.

The cuffs of your shirt should peek out from under the sleeve of your jacket about one-half an inch to no more than an inch when standing with your arms at your side. Button your cuffs; don't leave them unbuttoned unless you are not wearing a blazer and you plan on rolling them up. Many men avoid French cuffs today. These are the cuffs that require cuff links. They are a much more professional look. If you find a great shirt with French cuffs on the secondary market, give it a try. Those cuff links are probably buried somewhere in the bottom of your drawer or your brother's.

Shirts come in a wide range of colors and fabrics. (I am not talking about flannel shirts.) Start out with simple colors and patterns, and grow your collection as your income grows. No-iron shirts are easier to care for if they are removed promptly from the dryer. A little ironing is still a great idea. Golf shirts or three-button knit shirts are a step down in professional appearance but above t-shirts. Don't forget to tuck your shirt in to your pants.

Ties

Helping a man who has never tied a tie before choose a great tie and then tie it is my favorite part of *Men's Ready for Success*. This uniform accessory can be the most intimidating to some men. The colors and patterns are unlimited and can be overwhelming in the beginning. Search the secondary market for nice silk ties, and have fun with them.

I have taught tie tying to enthusiastic audiences of men and women. Search the back of the tie for two diagonal stitchings. These marks tell you where to center the back of the tie for the "average" man. Once you locate them they can guide you as to the placement of the tie to prevent the thin side (the back of the finished tie) from hanging out below the wider fat side (the front of the finished tie). I have included an illustration of the four-in-hand knot. I even have a little poem for you.

Place the fat over the thin
Do it again,
But put your thumb in
Then up, through
And under the chin
Down and under
Tighten with the thin.

Your tie should never hang below the waist of your pants. The point should hit at the middle of your belt. On the backside of most ties today is a label, where you can pull the thin side through to keep the two sides together. Men used to wear many styles of tie tacks and tie bars to do the same thing. Today they are less popular. I have noticed increasing interest in these items with the retro look.

There are many tying demonstrations on the Internet, though some are better than others. The width of ties changes with fashion, as do the size of the knot and the colors, so start simple.

Ties should never be left hanging already tied ready to be slipped over your neck and tightened. It is very hard on the silk; the dust will collect on the knot, and it no longer looks its best. Ties are best rolled up and put in dividers in drawers so they do not become crushed. Many men loop their ties over tubular hangers so they are easy to see.

If wearing a suit is too formal for the interview, at least wear a tie with a nice pair of pants and a dress shirt. A client returned to *Men's Ready for Success*. "Remember me?" he said. "I was here last month. I wanted to tell you I got the job you helped me get ready for. He hired me at my interview! He said I was the only person who came in wearing a tie. He said if I took that much care with getting ready for the interview, he was going to assume I would take that much care with my job. Thank you."

Sweaters and vests

Sweaters and vests are easy ways to expand your working wardrobe with little cost. They can be worn…

- under jackets.
- without jackets over shirts, to add warmth and style.
- with or without ties.

They are articles of men's clothing that can be found easily in the secondary market and on sale racks. Bulky sweaters are less desirable for work because of their suggestion of a casual Saturday afternoon at home.

Sweaters and sweater vests should be folded and put on closet shelves or in drawers. Hanging can cause uneven stretching and unsightly hanger bumps.

Shoes

Shoes can destroy a great image. Find the nicest leather shoes you can afford. Dressy lace shoes (unless they have gum soles) will be more conservative than slip-ons or loafers. Avoid wearing tennis shoes to work. They are only appropriate for fast-food jobs. Even then be sure they are clean, laced, and the laces are clean.

A little wipe down with Doc Marten's Wonder Balsam will keep your leather shoes looking new. Have at least two pairs of work shoes so you can alternate days of wearing. Please replace your laces when they break or before if they start to look frayed. No knots! For more tips on shoes, see Chapter 6.

Thick athletic socks will stretch out leather shoes. A men's dress sock in a thin fabric is a better choice for business. Dark socks with or without simple vague patterns are the most conservative. Some men like bright, fun socks, which is fine, except for the interview. Please avoid white socks at work unless your job requires work boots!

Hats

I added this short section because few men today seem to understand hats should be removed when indoors. I know many young men disagree with me. I was standing inside a restaurant when a young man dropped off his application. He was wearing his baseball cap as he handed the application to the cashier. I commented to the cashier how few young men remove their hats anymore. She laughed and said I'd be surprised at how many of them wore hats to interviews. When it was mentioned that they would not be allowed to wear hats at work, the young men were frequently shocked. Give yourself a head start on your competition—TAKE OFF YOUR HAT, even if you are just dropping off your application.

In Case You Missed It

Much of what I have to say to the women also applies to the men, so I've pointed out some important chapters for you to look over:

Chapter 6: "Shoes Are Not Thine Enemy!"
Chapter 7: "Keeping Up Appearances"
 Shaking Hands
 Your Hands
 Your Body
 Your Smile
 Your Body Piercings
 Your Tattoos
 Clothing Care
 Laundering Tips
 Dry Cleaning
 Using a Steamer
 Little Things that Count
 Button, Button, Who's Got the Button?
Chapter 9: "Organizing Your Closet to Save You Time and Money"
Chapter 10: "I Get the Idea, but I Still Can't Afford It!"

Epilogue

I can't tell you for sure how I knew a navy blazer would change my life, but it did! Little did I know that blazer would change the lives of others.

I was blessed to work with "Susan" on all three of her visits. The first was a cold January day. She had just finished a data entry course and was preparing for a job interview the next week. She was tall, Rubenesque, on public assistance, and the mother of three children. We talked about working, dressing for the workplace, dressing every day in an appropriate manner, and paying attention to what her female supervisors wore.

"Susan" got her job and revisited us on a hot day in June for summer wardrobe pieces. She said it was a lot of work to work! We all had a good laugh. But she was enjoying it and was pleased with her job and, mostly, with herself. In December she came back for a third and final visit. Pulling me aside she said, "Joyce, I was called in to the supervisor this morning. I was so nervous thinking about all the negative things that could happen: getting laid off at Christmas, getting fired! Instead I was told they would be starting a new position in January paying twice my current salary and they would like me to apply for it! Do you know what this means to me? One year ago I thought I would be a poor single mother forever—one more name on the welfare rolls for the rest of my life! Now I know I am more, and my children even treat me differently."

I didn't start out to change anyone's life except my own. I have learned that as I have presented myself differently to the world in the way I dress, the world has responded to me differently. As people came to expect and see me as a confident, capable woman, I began to see myself that way too. Don't get me wrong. I still have those nasty little gremlins occasionally running around in my head saying, "Who do you think you are? And who are you trying to impress?" But they are quieter and more respectful in their tone.

As I completed the first edition of this book, multiple sclerosis reared its ugly head and again forced me to re-examine my life with its challenges and limitations. I retired from *Ready for Success* in January of 2004. The seven years with this organization were an amazing journey. I was blessed to work with incredible women both as volunteers and clients. I love speaking to groups, and writing this book has been an astonishing experience. So, while my time with *Ready for Success* has ended, I don't think God is through with me yet. I look forward to doing what I have been doing, only with a wider audience—sharing with other women the strength of the woman looking back at each of us in the mirror.

On February 2, 2002, at 2:00 in the afternoon, I married a wonderful man. I did a much better job of choosing a life-partner this time! Life is good; that is not to say it is perfect. Few people have the opportunity to look at their life and say, "That was hard, but now I know why."

It seems like many, many years ago when I leaned against the shower wall and cried, *"Please God, help me out of this craziness. What do you want me to do?"* I hope I'm doing it.

Follow Your Dream: Tips for Starting a Non-Profit.

I have frequently been asked how I created a non-profit organization with no previous experience. In the first place, I had experience as a volunteer and a client in several areas of social service. Next, and most important, I didn't do it alone. A wonderful of group of individuals came forward and offered to help. Some offered their expertise in only a small piece of the puzzle but in important areas in which I had no experience (which, to be honest, was most areas), and some came forward and have stayed. So I became WE. We hope we developed a reputation for listening to other ideas. But to be honest, we were blessed with a very clear vision of what we wanted the program to accomplish and how we wanted the atmosphere and the environment to consider not only our clients but also our volunteers.

If you are interested in developing a non-profit, here are few tips I would like to share.

1. Decide you can do it! Take action!
2. Create a clear plan of what it is you want to accomplish; this could be a business plan or something that eventually will develop into a business plan. Consider these questions:

- Who will be the target audience of your organization?
- What do you want your audience to gain from exposure to the program?

3. Figure out who you know who could help you carry out your plan. A church group, a civic organization, a school group?

- Get a small committee involved early to create ownership in the program, and be open to their ideas and suggestions. Remember that everyone has gifts to share. *Ready for Success* was blessed with many wonderful, dedicated volunteers who stepped forward with their own gifts to share and create a team for action.

4. Determine whether your program is a new idea for your geographical area. Are there other programs in your area? How will yours be different? Is your idea based on a similar idea somewhere else? Can you talk with people involved in similar programs to hear about things they learned on their journey?

5. If your plan involves other agencies, get their comments early. They may have good suggestions and encouragement.

6. Learn everything you can about your field of interest, even the hard parts, which for me was learning to read a profit-and-loss statement.

7. Consider how the program will it be funded. The questions above are the same ones your potential funders will have, so be prepared.

Being a "social entrepreneur" has been an amazing experience. It is awe-inspiring to meet former clients who are now volunteers; enjoy the company of volunteers who have been on this path as long as I have; have a woman whisper in my ear at a place of business, *"I went to Ready for Success. That is how I got the clothes to get this job. Thank you"*; and sit at a fundraiser where a couple hundred men and women chose to support the program with their checkbooks. I encourage you to follow your heart and persist in following your dream. God's plan for me was greater than anything I ever imagined. Good Luck.

Resources

Products

Aihu Body and Home Care Products
www.aihu.net
I love this company's face lotion and under-eye crème. They have a wonderful mint massage lotion too.

Burt's Bees
www.burtsbees.com
I like the Lemon Butter Cuticle Cream.

Doc Marten's Wonder Balsam
www.drmartensforlife.com/for-life-products/care-instructions/
This is one of my favorite shoe care products.

Georgia's Girl Handbags
www.georgiasgirl-handbags.com
These are great handbags with an even greater purpose.

Hollywood Fashion Secrets
www.hollywoodfashionsecrets.com
Hollywood Fashion Tape can help keep your blouses from bulging out.

Trendy Tabs
www.trendytabs.com
These tabs can help you find your credit cards in a hurry.

Helpful Websites

Body Shape Calculator
www.shopyourshape.com/calculate-your-body-shape.html
Put in your measurements, and this site will tell you your body type and suggests clothing choices.

Men's Wearhouse
www.menswearhouse.com
This website has lots of wonderful tips on men's wear. Check out the Style Advice tab.

Paula Begoun
www.beautypedia.com and www.cosmeticscop.com
These websites are wonderful resources for beauty products for both men and women. There are some great tips on using products under the Learn tab.

The Happiness Project
www.happinessprojecttoolbox.com
Use the tools on this website to help you set goals, determine your values, and keep resolutions.

Organizations

Toastmasters
www.toastmasters.org
This organization will help you with your communication skills. This international organization is a wonderful resource for overcoming your fear of speaking.

The Women's Alliance
www.thewomensalliance.org
If you are interested in starting a program like Ready for Success in your area, The Women's Alliance is waiting to hear from you.

Bibliography

Saiki, Diana. "Building Opportunities: Dressing for Success," The Forum for Family and Consumer Issues 10, no. 2 (2005), www.ncsu.edu/ffci/publications/2005/v10-n2-2005-october/pa-2-building.php.

Strickler, Jeff. "The Case Against Stretching Earlobes." Star Tribune, January 24, 2012, www.startribune.com/lifestyle/137908688.html.

Glossary

Business Casual

This is a dress code that is the most difficult to explain. It is often easier to express what is not appropriate: beachwear, yard work clothing, suggestive clothing, exercise wear. Acceptable clothing should be clean, pressed, and suitable for contact with customers and other employees.

Career Casual

This term is usually used to define a dress code slightly more formal than business casual but not as formal as professional dress.

Professional Dress

This dress code requires jackets, pants, and appropriate accessories; in addition, woman may wear skirts and dresses. This term can be intermingled with conservative dress.

Casual Friday

Traditionally this day at the end of the workweek allows a step down in dress from what's required during the rest of the week. Employees should be careful not to cross over to total weekend wear, including anything dirty, torn, or worn out.

Weekend Wear

This is clothing that is more suitable for weekend activities or relaxing around the house.

Daywear

This entails the selection of clothing suitable for the job you have or are seeking, whether it's professional dress or business casual.

Datewear

This is clothing worn on an evening out, such as dance club wear or suggestive, provocative, or revealing clothing.

"Retro" Look

This is a style of dressing popular in another age, most likely mid-century modern.

20 Success Secrets

#1　Make your first impression count! Do you want to spend the rest of the interview climbing up out of the hole your first impression put you in?

#2　Shopping and spending are two different activities. No one checks your bank account before you walk in the door of a store.

#3　Sometimes our closest family and friends have the most trouble with our new look. We no longer fit their image of us. Ask yourself, who do you need to impress? Start with the face in the mirror!

#4　Just as you would not consider wearing a McDonald's uniform out on a date, the clothes you wear to work are probably not what you will wear out with your friends or around the house. Your work wardrobe is what you need to gain positive strokes at work.

#5　Choose a base color to work with. Black is probably the easiest and looks great on most women. (In hindsight I should have chosen black over navy when I began.)

#6　How can you sell yourself if you don't think you have anything to sell? You are worth this opportunity. Repeat this to yourself often.

#7　Almost everyone who has ever accepted a job or promotion thinks, "This is over my head and sooner or later they will find out that I don't really know what I am doing." Never let fear stop you from taking on a new challenge.

#8　Dress for your workplace. You are representing your employer by how you dress and present yourself—not your eligibility on the dating circuit.

#9   Accessories can add the "WOW!" to a simple outfit, but over-doing accessories can create the cartoonish appearance of a sitcom character! Choose one focal point!

#10   There is no real secret to wearing a scarf. Put it on. Decide what feels comfortable to you. Then carry it off with attitude! No fuss-ing or fidgeting allowed.

#11   Consider the image your shoes portray. Other women may admire a cute open-toed shoe with a lovely pedicure, but many men will view that attention to your feet as frivolous or even sexy. Is that how you want to be viewed in your workplace?

#12   Shoes last longer if you polish them regularly and rotate their use! Well-tended shoes say a lot about your attention to detail and concern about your appearance.

#13   The details matter! Whether you work in a professional setting or a more casual setting, the details of your personal appearance are important.

#14   Learn to shake hands firmly and positively! It is an important first impression. Many employers will judge you by your handshake.

#15   SMILE. Your smile is the most important thing you will put on for your interview and job! If you are not comfortable smiling around strangers, practice!

#16   If you get a tattoo, never put it where it can be seen in an in-terview.

#17   I have yet to meet a woman who thinks she has the perfect body, whether she is size 6, 12, 16, or 24. We waste too much time and energy obsessing about our bodies! Remember the ads with supermodels are even retouched. Let's move on, ladies!

#18   Hang the pieces to your suits separately. You will see them as separates with more choices of clothing partners within your closet.

#19   Don't buy it, no matter how great the deal is, if…

- it is the wrong size today even if you are on a diet.
- the color isn't good on you.
- it's the right size but a poor fit for your body type.
- it needs alterations, unless the store offers them for free or you do that type of thing regularly. Don't just add it to your pile to do someday.
- it is still more than your budget allows, unless you will wear it enough times to justify the cost.

#20   Sometimes a sale or bargain is not one! Do the math of a sale.

Head to Toe - Interview Ready

Dressing for the Interview
Tips from Joyce Nelson Shellhart,
author of
Dress to Impress: How a Navy Blazer Changed My Life

You only have a few seconds to make that first impression. Just remember how quickly you can flip through 200 TV channels and know there is nothing you want to watch. You want to be the station the employer pauses to consider.

First Things First

1. **Turn off your cell phone before you walk in the building!**

2. **Smile.** If you are not accustomed to smiling, practice! A sincere, honest smile lights up your face and adds a twinkle of interest to your eyes.

3. **Shake hands.** Practice, practice, practice on your friends, your family, and even strangers, so it is a natural movement for you in greeting. While shaking hands, smile, then exchange greetings— say your name and repeat the interviewer's name. Wear your name badge on your right shoulder so the interviewer's eye will naturally follow your hand to your written name.

Head-to-Toe

1. Head

• Make sure your hair is clean and neatly presented, not hanging in your eyes. Get a decent haircut.

- Women: Keep you make-up simple; this is not a date.
- Brush your teeth. There should be no gum or candy in your mouth
  - If you are trying to disguise cigarette breath, get rid of the candy or gum before you walk in the building for the interview.
- Wear only one earring in each ear; remove the facial piercings, especially on the tongue.

2. Tops

Men
- What is appropriate for the job? A suit would be too much for auto parts clerk but perfect for a banking professional. Should you wear a shirt and tie or a shirt, tie, and sport coat? Be sure they are clean and pressed. Wear a belt and tuck in your shirt. Dress one or two steps above your expected job.

Women
- What is appropriate for this particular job? Dress at least a step or two above for the interview. Remember the difference between daywear and datewear. Keep your jewelry simple and not distracting.

3. Hands

- Nails should be clean and filed.
- If you wear nail polish, it should not be chipped or either too dark or too bright.
- Keep your nails a reasonable length. Will the interviewer be wondering if you can use a keyboard with those nails, or if the tapping will bother other employees?

4. Bottoms

Men
- Make sure your pants are pressed, and if your pants drag on the ground, find a tailor.

Women
- Skirts and dresses should either be just above the knee or just below. Don't let your pants drag on the ground.

5. Shoes

- Your shoes will tell more about you than you know. Do you pay attention to details?
- Women: No open toes, no matter how pretty your pedicure.

Relax and concentrate on the interview.

About the Author

"Everyone should have the opportunity to learn or be present in Joyce Nelson Shellhart's presentation," commented a participant on a written evaluation following a Dress to Impress Workshop.

Joyce has appeared in front of hundreds of men and women speaking on the topic of dressing to impress. A caseworker called Joyce following one presentation and said, "After your appearance, a client asked if she could go home and change. She had an interview later in the day and did not feel she was dressed appropriately for it after hearing you speak."

Since retiring from Ready for Success, Joyce's Dress to Impress Workshops and motivational speaking "Life is an Amazing Journey – Go First Class or What is Keeping You in the Baggage Compartment?" has connected her with a wide variety of audiences: workforce centers, corporate meetings, networking events and women's conferences.

Joyce acknowledges each time she:

- is considered for a speaking event or workshop,
- steps in front an audience,
- is introduced as the author of Dress to Impress;

She is faced with the **"first impression"** of the interview. And sometimes she has to climb up out of the hole her appearance has put her in! Building her own business as an author and speaker opened her eyes to importance of presentation for even an entrepreneur. Joyce sees each interview as an opportunity polish her skills. She knows she has learned more from her mistakes, which she is not afraid to humorously share with her audiences. Information about her motivational speaking, workshop topics and availability can be found on her websites www.joycenelsonshellhart.com and www.dressingforwork.com.

She remains an avid cheerleader for the Ready for Success program and occasional volunteer. Several years as a family caregiver placed her directly in the 'peanut butter' of the "sandwich generation".

Joyce can be found wandering around department stores, consignment stores and thrift shops, occasionally with a grandchild in tow – teaching another generation the finer points of shopping.

Joyce Nelson Shellhart lives with her husband, Bruce in Minneapolis, Minnesota. They share their home with a black miniature poodle -Natalie, one Umbrella Cockatoo – Popcorn and a Ring-Neck Dove – MochaLatte.